BEAUTIFUL
BEADS

BEAUTIFUL BEADS

Alexandra Kidd

Chilton Book Company
Radnor, Pennsylvania

A Quarto Book

Copyright © 1994 Quarto Inc.

ISBN 0-8019-8629-X pb
ISBN 0-8019-8644-3 hb

Reprinted in 1995

A CIP record for this book is available from
the Library of Congress.

This book was designed and produced by
Quarto Inc.
The Old Brewery
6 Blundell Street
London N7 9BH

Editor Laura Washburn
Copy Editor Lydia Darbyshire
Senior Art Editor Nick Clark
Designer Debbie Mole
Illustrators Elsa Godfrey, Rob Shone
Photographer Paul Forrester
Art Director Moira Clinch
Editorial Director Sophie Collins

Typeset in Great Britain by Genesis Typesetting
Manufactured by Bright Arts Pte. Ltd., Singapore
Printed by Star Standard Industries Pte. Ltd., Singapore

INTRODUCTION 6

STRINGING 16

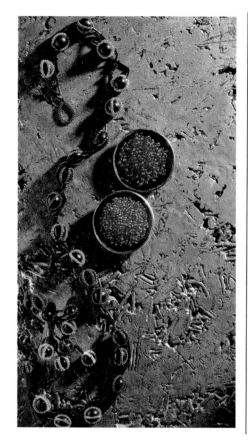

WIREWORK 40

Beads have been used around the world for almost as long as people have had the means to bore holes and to string materials together. Although the earliest beads were made from pieces of animal bone or horn, from shells or from seeds, it was not long before wood, pottery, metals, and glass were being used.

The Egyptians had magnificent jewels, both men and women wearing broad collars made from beads strung in many rows, and Tutankhamen was buried in a ceremonial apron made of gold plates inlaid with multicolored glass and threaded with bead borders. Beads were made in China during the Bronze Age, and the Romans used glass to make beads. Etruscan tombs have revealed necklaces, brooches, bracelets, and rings, and archeological finds from Syria have included pottery beads dating from the 5th–10th centuries.

Today, beads are still made all over the world. Go into almost any craft shop or the notions department of a large store and you will find hundreds of different kinds, shapes, and colors of bead made from wood, glass, semiprecious stones, coral, metal, pottery, and, of course, plastic, which will have been treated in so many ways that it is almost unrecognizable.

INTRODUCTION

Small crystal and glass beads

Cut crystal beads

GLASS BEADS Glass is perhaps the most versatile medium for beads. Many of the projects in this book use the little glass beads known as rocailles and bugles. These are available in dozens of colors and a variety of sizes – the smallest ones are often used for embroidery while the larger ones can be used as spacer beads. Opaque rocailles are ideal for loomwork and woven projects, and they can be used to recreate native American patterns. Rocailles and bugles can be transparent, iridescent, or opaline. Some are silver-lined, which makes them reflect light, others have metallic or pearl finishes. They used to be sold by weight, and they

Venetian millefiori beads

are still sometimes sold in long strings. Today, however, you are more likely to find them in small packets.

At the other end of the scale from the single-color rocailles and bugles are the wonderfully elaborate millefiori beads. These originated in the Venetian glassworks at Murano, where the technique was used to fuse together tiny multicolored canes of glass to create the highly patterned beads.

Lampwork beads – that is, beads made from molten glass – are now made all over the world. Millefiori beads are made in India and exported to the West, while in central Europe molten glass is used to cover small pieces of foil or even minute glass flowers to produce exquisite beads. Other lampwork beads are made with two or more colors wound together to create spiral effects, or contain spirals of fine metal wire. Sometimes two-color beads are ground so that the underlying color is revealed.

In the late 19th century, Daniel Swarovski developed a method of refining and cutting glass to create faceted beads, and this revolutionized the bead industry. Now many faceted glass beads are made by molding, and they are, of course, much cheaper than hand-cut beads. Nevertheless, they still sparkle and reflect the light, just as the more expensive hand-cut beads do.

Africa has specialized in the production of beads, called ground glass beads, from recycled glass, including old soft-drink bottles. These have an opaque finish and are often two- or even three-colored. We have used these for the necklace on pages 32–33.

WOOD Wooden beads are among the oldest type to have been made. In Japan and China wooden beads were elaborately carved, often with representational flowers and figures. Elsewhere wood has been simply smoothed and polished so that the natural grain and color can be appreciated. Yew, holly, oak, walnut, and boxwood have all been used in Europe, while hardwood beads, including those made from mahogany and tulipwood, have been produced in the Americas.

Wooden beads

Painted wooden beads

Metal beads

Decorative metal beads

Textured metal beads

METAL Gold and silver beads have been used for millennia to form decorations for kings and princes, and precious metals are, of course, still used today to make beads. Now, however, you are more likely to see beads made from base metals or even recycled saucepans.

Although they are not made in sterling silver, but in a silver alloy, beads from the Indian subcontinent are available in a range of traditional shapes and patterns. Filigree beads, which may be made as openwork pieces or with the decoration laid over a solid base, have been made throughout Europe, with the metal wire twisted into abstract and floral motifs in both gold and silver. Hammered metals, especially copper, have been used to create textured surfaces.

As with glass, recycling methods now mean that it is possible to find beads made from old saucepans or even motor parts. These often originate from Africa or the Far East.

CERAMIC Pottery beads were among the earliest forms of decoration to be made, and today ceramic beads are still made. Plain ceramic beads, such as those made in the UK, are sometimes formed into twisted cones or bicones, and brightly colored annular beads, dyed with metal oxides, are produced in Greece.

Often, however, ceramic beads are highly glazed and decorated. In Greece there is a tradition of decorating hand-rolled beads with pretty floral motifs, while beads from China will have painted flowers outlined in metallic finishes. Peruvian beads are often decorated with intricately hand-painted scenes and patterns.

Plain ceramic beads

Painted ceramic beads

Lapis lazuli beads

Turquoise beads

SEMIPRECIOUS STONES Agate, jade, lapis lazuli, turquoise – the variety of semiprecious stones that can be formed into beads is almost unlimited, and they offer the opportunity to make some lovely pieces. Try alternating semiprecious beads with silver or gold beads to create some exquisitely simple necklaces. Because these beads tend to be expensive, they are best strung on sturdy thread with a knot between each bead. This helps to prevent the beads from being lost if the thread breaks (see the project on pages 28–29).

Amber and jet, which are not true stones, can also be used alone or in combination with gold and silver spacers and findings to make traditionally styled pieces. Amber is really the fossilized gum from coniferous trees, and its color ranges from rich red to yellow. Jewelry made from jet, a mineral similar to lignite, has been found in Bronze Age tombs, and it was enormously popular in Britain in the 19th century.

Jet beads

NATURAL MINERALS Beads from natural materials such as bone, horn (including ivory), and seeds are less likely to be encountered today, unless you find old pieces of jewelry in antique and thrift stores and decide to give them a new lease on life by restringing them or by reusing the beads in a new way.

Shell beads are still made, however. Mother-of-pearl is sometimes carved into pendants and beads, while both mother-of-pearl and abalone are often inlaid as decoration into plain beads.

Coral beads

Pearls and coral have long been highly valued as beads, and both may be too expensive for everyday use. The wide-scale production of cultured pearls and modern manufacturing methods that have made possible the production of glass imitation pearls and pearlized plastics have brought pearl or pearl-like beads within the reach of all beaders. While these imitations can never emulate the beautiful luster of real pearls, they offer the beader scope to create some traditional pieces that would otherwise not be possible.

With so many different beads to choose from it is sometimes difficult to know where to begin.

When you are making simple earrings, bracelets, and necklaces with beads of just one color, try adding a few silver or gold spacer beads or rondels in between to give them extra sparkle and to personalize them.

Traditional African or Native American designs can be worked in any colors or combinations of colors you like, although the beads should be all more or less the same size. If you use widely different sizes the piece will be uneven. Choose the color combinations carefully — if the tones are too close it will be impossible to see the pattern clearly. If your pattern has three colors, choose a light, a medium and a dark shade. If you are unsure about your choice, work some small samples with different colors before you embark on a major project.

DESIGN FUNDAMENTALS

Traditional beadwork patterns are normally made with opaque rocailles in primary colors. If you use silver-lined or transparent rocailles instead, you will get a completely different effect.

If you are lucky enough to have some beautifully decorated, elaborately patterned beads – perhaps some that you have made from polymer clay (see pages 12–13) – use them with just one other color of plain bead. If you introduce too many different colors or shapes you will overwhelm the impact of the special beads and distract attention from their beauty.

Each project in this book has a Materials list at the beginning to help you organize all the equipment needed to make the piece. These lists are specific to the projects but there are a number of items that are useful for most beadwork, such as fine beading needles, beading thread, eye pins and head pins, and round-nosed pliers.

It is also helpful to have a few basic findings — the items that transform beads into pieces of jewelry. Findings include earring hooks, brooch backs, calotte crimp beads, bell tips, spacer bars, and clasp fittings. Many bead suppliers sell most of the findings necessary to bead jewelry.

1 Earring wires and hoops
2 Earring findings
3 Jump rings and triangles
4 Spacer beads
5 Rhinestone clasps
6 Pierced ear posts
7 Necklace clasps
8 End tips
9 Calotte crimp beads
10 Leather connectors
11 Perforated brooch bases
12 Brooch backs
13 Head pins and eye pins

For more variety, beads can also be decorated or made at home. Most craft stores stock unvarnished wooden beads; avoid varnished beads because the paint will not adhere satisfactorily. Use acrylic paints and apply a coat of clear varnish once the paint is dry.

There are several types of polymer clay available under a range of proprietary brandnames. They are all, however, basically the same, varying only in the range of colors offered and the degree of malleability. Plain polymer clay beads can be decorated with acrylic paints, which can be applied before or after baking. You can also use water-based paints, but they may not cover as well, although you will achieve some interesting effects, and they are well worth experimenting with. There are also the colorful fabric paints, including glitter finishes, that are sold for decorating T-shirts, and these can be used, again either before or after baking.

Baking times vary slightly by brand, so always check the packet. Because over- or under-baking can ruin the finished item and

HOMEMADE BEADS

SAFETY FIRST

•

Polymer clays give off noxious fumes. Always work in a well-ventilated room, and, as an additional precaution, do not leave children or pets (including birds) in the kitchen while you are baking your clay beads. The plasticizer in unbaked clays leaches out, so do not store or work with clay in or with utensils and containers that you use for food preparation. As a further precaution, do not use articles made of clay, even when it has been baked, to store or serve food. Always wash your hands thoroughly after you have been working with polymer clay.

because different ovens cook in different ways, it is best to utilize an oven thermometer so that you can find the optimum temperature within your oven for obtaining an even, accurate result. It is also sensible to experiment with sample pieces before you expend a lot of time and effort on something really special, only to find that it is ruined in the oven.

Make the holes in the beads before baking. A small knitting needle or wooden skewer may be appropriate for some of your beads, while others will need a much finer tool. You will make neater holes if you insert the tool from one side and then from the other so that the two holes meet in the middle. If you take your piercing tool right through you will have to rub away any rough edges that are formed by the tool as it emerges on the other side.

PAINTED WOODEN BEADS

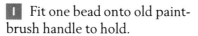

For the ultimate in individuality, decorate an assortment of wooden beads using colored and metallic paints.

YOU WILL NEED
•

- Plain wooden beads, untreated
- Acrylic paints
- Clear varnish
- Paintbrushes in various sizes
- Wooden skewer or knitting needle
- Old paintbrush handle to fit holes in beads
- Leather thong, cord, or ribbon
- Fastener

1 Fit one bead onto old paint-brush handle to hold.
2 Paint base color with a large brush.

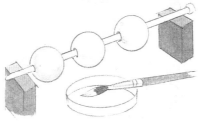

3 Slide the painted bead onto a skewer or knitting needle and leave to dry.
4 Repeat steps 1–3 with the remaining beads.

Plain coconut shell beads can also be painted and strung closely together for a dramatic effect.

5 When the base coat is dry, slide the beads back onto the paint-brush handle used in step 1 and decorate as desired. Leave to dry between colors.
6 When all beads have been decorated and are completely dry, cover with an even coat of varnish and leave to dry. Assemble the necklace.

Match the color of the leather thong to the tones of the painted beads.

USING POLYMER CLAY

Imaginative use of colors will result in some stunning polymer beads. More sophisticated techniques are explained here but you could also begin by making plain beads.

Marbled polymer beads

YOU WILL NEED

•

For the marbled beads
- 2–3 different colors of polymer clay
- Rolling pin
- Craft knife
- Piercing needle

For the millefiori beads
- 5–6 different colors of polymer clay
- Rolling pin
- Craft knife
- Piercing needle

MARBLED BEADS

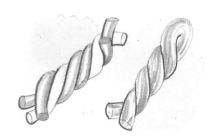

1 Take the clays and knead them together. Stop kneading before the colors blend completely to make a new color and at a point when you can still see distinct colors.

2 Roll out the clay to form a sausage-shape that is about ½ inch thick.
3 Use a craft knife to cut the sausage into equal pieces and roll the pieces in the palms of your hands to create evenly sized, smooth balls.
4 Pierce a hole through the beads and bake according to the manufacturer's instructions.

White polymer clay adds brightness to marbled beads.

3 Repeat step 2 with another color, but do not wrap another color around the roll. Cut it into five even pieces.

Polymer millefiori beads

6 Make base beads from a plain color clay, rolling the small pieces in the palms of your hands to form smooth balls.

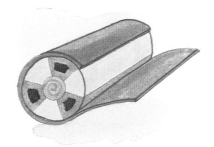

4 Assemble the millefiori cane by placing the spiral in the center. Arrange the other pieces around it, alternating the two kinds. Gently press them together.

7 Cover each ball with millefiori slices, pressing them gently together but taking care not to squash the balls. Leave to rest for a few hours before baking according to the manufacturer's instructions.

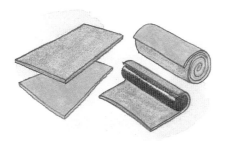

Combine polymer beads with small ceramic beads and colored threads.

MILLEFIORI BEADS

1 Roll out two sheets of differently colored clay until they are ⅛ inch thick and place one on top of the other. Roll together so that they look like a jelly roll.

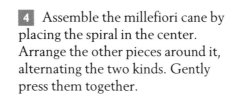

5 Wrap the whole cane in another sheet of clay and carefully roll it out until it is about ¼ inch in diameter. Use your craft knife to cut thin slices from the cane. You should discard the two ends, which will be somewhat misshapen.

2 Take a third color and use your hands to roll it into a long, thin sausage-shape, about 1 inch in diameter. Roll out another colour into a sheet about ⅛ inch thick and wrap this around the sausage-shape. Carefully roll this with your hands to create a longer, thinner sausage-shape. Cut the shape into five even pieces.

Millefiori beads can be as long or short as you like.

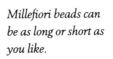

STRINGING

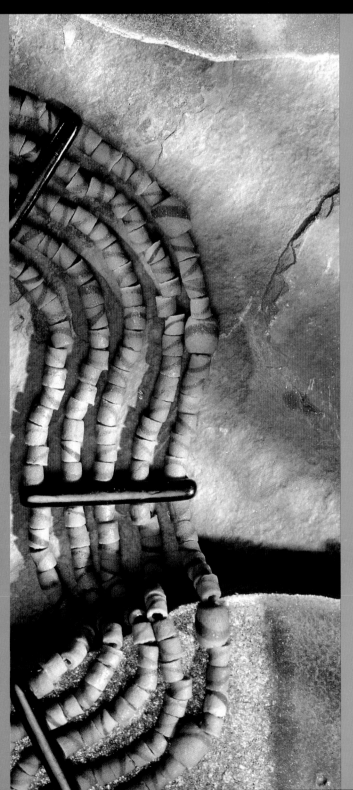

T here is a lot more to stringing than simply putting beads on thread. The following is a list of the basics, but don't forget that you can also string beads on colorful hanks of embroidery silks, rubber tubing, very fine chains, ribbons, and furnishing cords. Yours is the inspiration!

TYPES OF STRING There are many different levels of bead stringing or threading and a good place to start is by stringing large, bright beads onto elastic for simple bracelets. Use two knots and glue the knot inside a large bead to secure it.

Leather can also be used for simple threading. It is an excellent way to show off a few special beads, or to string large, heavy beads, if they have fairly wide holes. You can buy round leather thonging in bead shops or leather shoelaces in shoe stores. Don't forget to check the size of the holes in your beads before you buy them. The simplest way to use leather is to string your beads, perhaps knotting either side of the pattern for safety, then thread both ends of the leather through a wide, strong bead and knot the ends of the thong.

Fig. 1

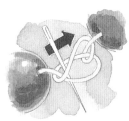

Fig. 2

More sophisticated levels of stringing use nylon monofilament, which can be bought in bead shops or as fishing line (ask for a weight between 12 and 20 pounds, depending on your beads). Nylon line is very good for cheap, cheerful beads, but it doesn't hang very elegantly. It doesn't need to be threaded with a needle, but it does have to be fastened with French crimp beads. Leave a small gap, about ¼ inch, between your beads and the clasp, because nylon monofilament tends to shrink over time.

Tiger tail is a specialist thread for stringing. It is composed of fine strands of steel cable encased in a plastic coating. Again, it needs to be attached to the fastener with French crimp beads. Tiger tail is a good, all-purpose string and is especially useful for heavy beads. It is very strong for its diameter, but it is not recommended for use with lighter beads as it doesn't hang well and can kink easily.

For more specialist stringing, there are nylon cords, polyester threads, and silk threads. All of these can be either crimped to the fastener, knotted, or used with a calotte.

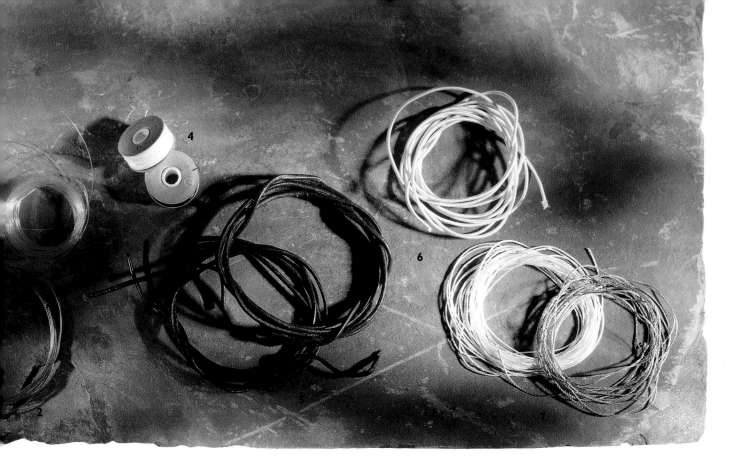

Polyester can be bought ready-waxed, which makes it easy to string without needles. It does stretch over time, so leave your work to hang for a few days, especially if you are using heavy beads, before you finish your second end. Silk can be bought on cards with a needle worked into the end; this is fairly expensive but excellent for fine beads. Nylon cord can be used with a needle, or by stiffening the end. To do this, dip the end into clear nail polish.

KNOTTING This is most often used at the ends of a necklace, to secure the final bead and the clasp fitting, or it can be used as a decorative or protective feature between beads (*fig. 1*). When a large knot, or a more secure knot, is required, use a double knot (*fig. 2*).

EQUIPMENT The equipment necessary for stringing includes a good pair of pliers, either flat-nosed or round-nosed, for attaching clasps and other findings. Beading needles can be bought in a hobby pack of different sizes. You will also need sharp scissors, and for knotting you will need some fine-pointed, curved tweezers and something to put into your knots — opened paper clips are fine. It is also a good idea to have extra wax when you are using thread to help with the stringing.

FINISHING OFF Always leave a 3 inch tail of thread when tying your first knot. After stringing all the beads, run the tail back through several beads, then cut. Never cut thread next to a knot as this will weaken the knot. A dab of clear nail polish comes in handy for securing knots. Another way to finish a necklace is with a knot and a calotte crimp bead. Be careful not to let the calotte cut the thread when doing this!

1 *Decorative cord*
2 *Tiger tail*
3 *Nylon monofilament*
4 *Beading thread*
5 *Leather thongs*
6 *Elastic cord*
7 *Silk thread*

SIMPLE STRINGING

Beads on a string is about as simple as jewelry making gets, but creative mixing and matching results in some truly stunning necklaces.

YOU WILL NEED
•

Beads and findings for the single strands
- About 4–5 ounces assorted small beads
- Beading thread
- Beading needle

Other equipment
- Scissors

Beads and findings for the multi-strand
- Approximately 26 large beads
- Approximately 29 medium beads
- Approximately 500 small beads
- 2 × round bell tips
- 2 × conical bell tips
- 2 × jump rings
- I large hook
- Feature pendant (we used one in the shape of a human figure)
- Beading needle
- Beading thread

Other equipment
- Scissors
- Clear nail polish

MAKING THE SINGLE STRANDS

1 Take a length of thread through the needle and double it to make a length of about 36 inches. Begin picking up beads at random until you have threaded about 31½ inches of beads.

2 Bring the two ends together and tie a knot close to the beads. Run the ends back through a few beads before cutting off.

3 Repeat steps 1–2 to make three more strands.

MAKING THE MULTI-STRAND

1 Take a long length of thread, using it double and leaving a tail of about 6 inches. Pick up a random selection of small, medium and large beads until the line is about 24 inches long. Leave a tail of about 6 inches at the other end and set aside.

2 Repeat step 1 but use mainly medium and large beads.

3 Make a third strand in the same way but use mainly small and medium beads.

4 Make two more strands but use only small beads.

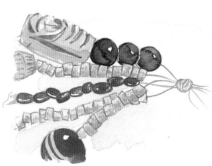

5 Join the ends of the five strands together with two knots tied close to the beads.

6 Run the threads through a round bell tip, then a conical bell tip, take the thread around the clasp and wrap it around several times. Take the thread back through both bell tips and tie a knot around the first cluster of knots. Take the threads back through the beads before cutting off. Dab a spot of nail polish on the knots. Repeat at the other end, attaching a jump ring instead of the clasp.

7 Use a jump ring to attach the pendant to one of the strands of small beads.

Multi-strand necklaces can also be made from a single type of bead. Dress one up by wrapping it with the four single strands.

MOON & STARS NECKLACE

*This simple necklace uses the basic techniques for stringing
beads and attaching a fastener. We have added an attractive
pendant detail as a variation on the standard round necklace.*

YOU WILL NEED

•

Beads and findings
• 4 calotte crimp beads
• I snap fastener
• 5 rocaille beads, size 12/0
• 46 × 5mm glass beads
• 44 ceramic tube beads
• 7 oval patterned glass beads
• 3 flat patterned glass beads
• Tiger tail

Other equipment
• Scissors
• Round-nosed pliers
• Sewing needle (optional)

MAKING THE NECKLACE

1 Thread two of the calottes onto a length of tiger tail and pick up the loop of the fastener. Thread the tiger tail back through the calottes and squeeze them with your pliers.

2 Pick up a rocaille, a 5mm bead, another rocaille, and another 5mm bead, then pick up a tube bead.

3 Pick up a 5mm bead, two tube beads, a 5mm bead, and a tube bead. Repeat this step five times more.

4 Pick up one 5mm bead, one oval bead, one 5mm bead, and one tube bead. Repeat twice more so that you have three oval beads, separated by a 5mm bead, a tube bead, and a 5mm bead.

5 Pick up one 5mm bead, one flat bead, two 5mm beads, one flat bead, one 5mm bead, one oval bead, and a rocaille.

6 Take the tiger tail back through the oval bead, 5mm bead, flat bead, and one of the 5mm beads, leaving the rocaille on a loop. To stop the thread becoming too tight, place a needle through the loop.

7 Push all the beads you have picked up so far back up toward the fastener and pull the tiger tail taut, making sure that it does not get twisted.

8 Pick up beads to match the first side, ending with a rocaille.

9 Pick up two calottes and take the tiger tail through the loop on the fastener. Take the tiger tail back through the calottes and squeeze them firmly. Cut off the end of the tiger tail.

For the matching earrings, you will need 12 silver beads, 2 × 5mm glass beads, 2 flat patterned glass beads, 2 silver star beads, 2 silver moon beads, 6 eye pins, and 2 earring hooks. See pages 42–43 for wireworking instructions.

RED & BLUE STRANDED SET

Opaque rocailles are easily obtainable, but it is worth spending a little extra time to find really stunning large beads as the focal point of this project.

MAKING THE NECKLACE

1 Take about 55 inches of thread on a needle and fold the thread double so that the needle is in the center. Tie a knot.

2 Pick up one blue rocaille and about 6 inches of red rocailles. Cut one of the threads where it meets the needle and leave the loose thread aside.

3 Pick up one blue rocaille, one large blue bead, one blue rocaille, and about 16 red rocailles.

4 Repeat step 3 twice more, then pick up one blue rocaille, one large blue bead, and one blue rocaille. You will have four large blue beads separated by three groups of blue and red rocailles.

5 Return to the free thread and repeat step 3 three times.

6 Take the working thread through the final large blue bead and rocaille, then rejoin the threads on the needle. Pick up about 6 inches of red rocailles and one blue rocaille.

7 Repeat steps 1–6 twice more.

8 You will have six threads at each end. Pass these through a large-holed bead, then through a piece of gimp. On one side, go around the loop on the hook. On the other side, go around a jump ring. Pass the threads on both sides back through the large-holed bead.

9 Separate the ends of thread into two groups of three and tie two knots. Secure with a drop of glue. Leave to dry, then trim.

MAKING THE EARRINGS

1 Fasten a 20-inch length of thread to a jump ring, leaving a tail of about 4 inches. Pick up one blue rocaille and one large blue bead.

YOU WILL NEED
•

Beads and findings
- ½ ounce blue rocaille beads, size 8/0
- 2½ ounces red rocaille beads, size 8/0
- 6 × 10mm blue beads
- 2 large-holed metal beads
- 3 jump rings
- Hook or bolt ring
- 2 × ½ inch gimp
- 1 pair of earring hooks
- Beading needle
- Beading thread

Other equipment
- Scissors
- Clear, all-purpose glue

2 Pick up one blue rocaille, about 17 red rocailles, one blue rocaille, and one red rocaille. Miss the last three beads and take the thread back up through all the beads to the jump ring.

3 Loop the thread around the jump ring and take it through the blue rocaille and the large blue bead. Repeat step 2.

4 Repeat until you have four tassels, but on the last tassel take the thread only up to the top blue rocaille.

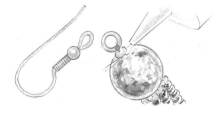

5 Thread the tail through the blue rocaille and fasten the two ends with two knots, securing with a drop of glue. When the glue is dry trim the ends neatly and attach the earring hook to the jump ring. Repeat for the other earring.

TASSEL NECKLACE

*We have made this 1930s-style necklace fairly long, although
you could easily shorten it by omitting two groups of bugles.
Use antique beads for a more authentic effect.*

MAKING THE STRANDS

1 Cut a 100 inch length of thread
and take through a needle. Pick up
one pink facet bead, one purple
rocaille, and about 6 inches of
bugles.

2 Pick up one blue rocaille, one
purple rocaille, one pink facet bead,
one long facet bead, one pink facet
bead, one purple rocaille, one blue
rocaille, and 2 inches of bugles.

3 Repeat step 2 three times more
so that you have four long facet
beads and four short lengths of
bugles.

4 Pick up one blue rocaille, one
purple rocaille, one pink facet bead,
and the large round bead.

*The finished length
of the necklace, from
the back point to the
bottom of the tassel,
is about 23¼ inches.*

5 Pick up one purple rocaille, 10
bugles, five rocailles (alternating
blue and purple), take the thread
back up through the bugles and the
purple rocaille.

6 Repeat step 5 once more and
take the thread back through the
large round bead and the pink facet
bead.

YOU WILL NEED
•

Beads and findings
- 18 × 6mm pink facet beads
- ⅛ ounce purple rocaille beads, size
  10/0
- 1 ounce 7mm black metallic bugles
- ⅛ ounce pale blue rocaille beads,
  size 10/0
- 8 long facet beads
- 1 large round bead
- Beading thread
- Beading needles

Other equipment
- Scissors
- Clear, all-purpose glue

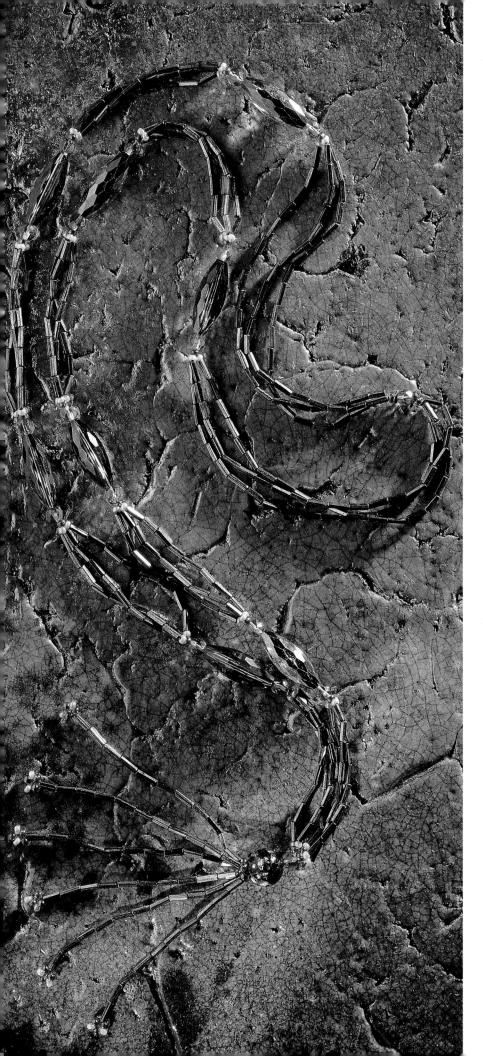

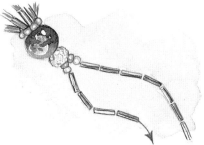

7 Working up the next side of the necklace, pick up one purple rocaille, one blue rocaille, about 2 inches bugles, one blue rocaille, one purple rocaille, one pink facet bead, one long facet bead, and one pink facet bead.

8 Repeat step 7 three times more.

9 Pick up one purple rocaille, one blue rocaille, about 6 inches bugles, and one purple rocaille.

10 Repeat the whole sequence twice more, but instead of picking up a new group of purple rocaille, pink facet bead, long facet bead, pink facet bead and purple rocaille each time, take the thread through the existing beads.

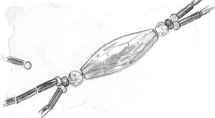

11 When all the strands are complete, take all the threads through the first pink facet bead. Tie two knots, one on each side of the bead, and secure with a spot of glue. Leave to dry before trimming the loose ends.

27

KNOTTED NECKLACE

The knotting technique is ideal for more costly beads, such as the semiprecious ones used here. Be sure to test the needle and thread for fit as semiprecious beads often have small holes.

YOU WILL NEED
•

Beads and findings
- 1 necklace clasp
- 24 × 8mm mother-of-pearl beads
- 19 × 10mm amazonite beads
- 14 × 9mm enameled bead caps
- Waxed polyester or silk thread
- Beading needle
  Other equipment
- Blunt-ended needle
- Fine-pointed, curved tweezers
- Instant adhesive

MAKING THE NECKLACE

1 Take a piece of thread about 50 inches long. Although this is more than you will need, it is difficult to join in a thread if you run out part way along a necklace.

2 Tie a simple knot about 4 inches from one end and insert a blunt-ended needle through the knot to hold it open. Thread on one part of the clasp, leaving about ½ inch between the clasp and the holding knot.

3 Make a first knot close to the clasp, then make five more knots until you reach the holding knot. Use fine tweezers to pull the end through each knot.

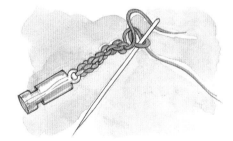

4 Thread the short end through the holding needle and pull it through the knot. Put a spot of adhesive on the end. Thread on a mother-of-pearl bead and try to get the short end through the bead too, although this is not essential.

5 Make the knot in the working thread and insert the blunt-ended needle through the knot. Hold the bead close to the row of knots with one hand and use the same hand to draw the knot with the needle toward the bead. At the same time, pull gently on the working thread with your other hand. When the knot is as close as possible to the mother-of-pearl bead, withdraw the needle from the knot, remembering to pull on the long end as you do so. If the knot is not sufficiently close to the bead, undo it carefully with your tweezers and redo it. Repeat twice more.

6 Thread on an amazonite bead and another mother-of-pearl bead, tying knots between each bead. Repeat five times more (you will have threaded 15 beads in all).

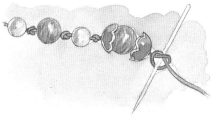

7 Continue to work in this way, alternating amazonite and mother-of-pearl beads, but pick up bead caps around the next seven amazonite beads. Work to the end to match the first half of the necklace.

8 Tie a knot after the last mother-of-pearl bead and leave the needle in it. Pick up the other part of the clasp, leaving about ½ inch between it and the last knot. Make a knot to attach the clasp, then make five more knots, as in step 3. Thread the working end through the holding needle and pull it through the knot. Put a drop of adhesive over the last knot and, if possible, thread the working end through the next bead. Cut the ends neatly when the glue is dry.

These matching earrings are made with a long eye pin and small silver beads, see pages 42–43 for wireworking techniques.

DESERT CHOKER

The finished length of this choker is about 12 inches without the clasp. To determine the right size, measure your neck and add or subtract the smaller beads as needed.

YOU WILL NEED
•

Beads and findings
- 1 × 1¼ inch perforated base
- 1 × 10mm silver bead
- 36 turquoise rocaille beads, size 6/0
- 27 black ceramic beads, approximately 4 × 5mm
- 30 turquoise rocaille beads, size 8/0
- 22 × 4mm black beads
- 3 × 25mm bone pipe beads
- 12 silver French crimp beads
- 12 × 50mm bone pipe beads
- 2 × 3-strand silver spacer bars
- 6 × 3mm silver beads
- 1 × 3-strand silver clasp
- 5 feet fishing line (monofilament)
- 3 feet tiger tail
- Beading needle

Other equipment
- Flat-nosed pliers

DECORATING THE NECKLACE

1 Thread the needle with the fishing line. You may find this easier to do if you squeeze the end of the line with the pliers to flatten.

2 Bring the thread up through one hole in the perforated base and down through another. Tie the thread at the back, leaving a tail.

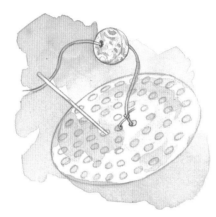

3 Attach the 10mm silver bead to the center of the base by bringing the thread to the front through an off-center hole. Pick up the bead and take the thread back through another off-center hole.

4 Bring the thread through a hole in the next circle. Pick up three 6/0 rocailles, laying them flat against the central bead. Take the thread down the next nearest hole and bring it back up about midway between the three beads. Take the thread through one of the beads. Repeat this step until you have completed the circle.

5 Bring the thread through a hole in the next row. Pick up two black ceramic beads, laying them along the edge of the previous circle of turquoise rocailles. Go down through the next nearest hole and bring the thread back up between the two black beads. Take the thread through one of the beads, then continue to add the black beads all the way around. Sew one 8/0 turquoise rocaille between each black bead.

6 Use 4mm black beads for the final row. Sew these on in the same way as the ceramic beads.

7 Finish off by tying the working thread and tail securely together and threading each through about three beads before cutting off.

MAKING THE DROPS

1 To make the central drop, take a new length of fishing line and bring it through one of the holes in the edge of the base. Pick up one 6/0 turquoise rocaille, one black ceramic bead, one 6/0 rocaille, one 25mm bone pipe, one 6/0 rocaille, one ceramic bead, one 6/0 rocaille and three 8/0 rocailles. Miss the last three beads and take the thread back through the others up to the perforated base.

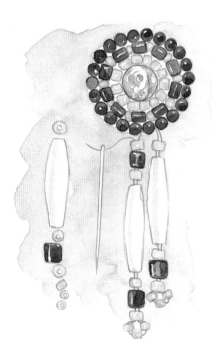

2 Pick up one 6/0 rocaille, one ceramic bead, one 6/0 rocaille, one 50mm pipe bead, and one 8/0 rocaille. Run the tiger tail through the middle of the spacer bar, then pick up one 6/0 rocaille, one ceramic bead, one 50mm pipe bead, one 3mm silver bead, and one crimp. Loop the tiger tail through the central hole in the clasp, thread it back through the crimp bead and pull it tightly. Squeeze the crimp bead. Repeat on the other side of the perforated base.

3 Take a new length of tiger tail and, counting two holes up from the centre of the base, loop it through and secure with a crimp. Pick up one 6/0 rocaille, one 50mm pipe bead, one 8/0 rocaille, one 6/0 rocaille, one ceramic bead, one 6/0 rocaille, and one 8/0 rocaille. Thread the tiger tail through the top hole of the spacer bar. Pick up one 6/0 rocaille, one ceramic bead, one 6/0 rocaille, one 50mm pipe bead, one 3mm silver bead, and a crimp bead. Loop the tiger tail through the top hole of the clasp and back through the crimp bead. Squeeze to close. Repeat on the other side.

4 Repeat step 3 but starting two holes down from the center of the base and using the bottom holes in the spacer bars and clasp.

2 Bring the thread out through the next hole in the base and make the next drop, following the diagram. When you have finished the second drop, take the thread to the hole on the other side of the central drop to make the third drop to match the second.

MAKING THE STRANDS

1 For the central strand, pick up a crimp bead with a length of tiger tail and loop it through a central hole along one edge of the base. Take the tiger tail back through the crimp bead and squeeze it closed with a pair of pliers.

GROUND GLASS NECKLACE

We used black spacer bars and black beads with these pretty African ground glass beads, which are stunning and the perfect choice for this five-strand showcase.

The top strand, with two sections of 16 beads and two sections of 12 beads, measures about 13½ inches.

Remember that any adjustments for size need to be carried over to each strand.

MAKING THE NECKLACE

1 Working with a long piece of double thread go through the top hole of one of the spacer bars, leaving a tail of thread. Pick up four black rocailles, one 8mm black bead, three black rocailles, one 8mm black bead, and one black rocaille. Miss the last rocaille and take the thread back through all.

2 Pick up 16 5mm beads, go through the second spacer, pick up 12 5mm beads and go through the third spacer. Pick up 12 5mm beads and go through the fourth spacer. Pick up 16 5mm beads and pick up the last spacer.

3 Pick up about 23 rocailles to form a loop. Check that the loop will fit over the 8mm beads, then take the thread back through the first two rocailles and through the spacer bar.

4 Run the thread back through all the beads to the tail. Tie the ends securely together, run each thread through three beads and cut off.

5 Begin the second row by going through the spacer bar, picking up a rocaille and going back through the spacer bar.

6 Pick up 17 5mm beads, go through the second spacer bar, pick up 14 5mm beads in the next two sections, then pick up 17 5mm beads in the last section.

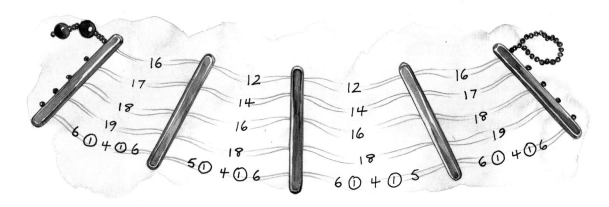

7 Go through the last spacer bar, pick up a rocaille, take the thread back through the spacer bar and through all the other beads. Finish off the ends as in step 4.

8 Thread the third row in the same way as the second, but pick up 18 beads in the two outside sections and 16 beads in the two inner sections.

9 Thread the fourth row in the same way as the second and third, but pick up 19 beads in the two outside sections and 18 beads in the two inner sections.

10 For the first section of the fifth row, begin as in step 5, but pick up six 5mm beads, one medium bead, four 5mm beads, one 8mm bead, and six 5mm beads.

11 Pick up five 5mm beads, one 8mm bead, four 5mm beads, one 8mm bead, and six 5mm beads. Reverse the order for the second inner section, so that the six 5mm beads are next to the central spacer bar. Complete the last section as in step 10. Finish off as in step 4.

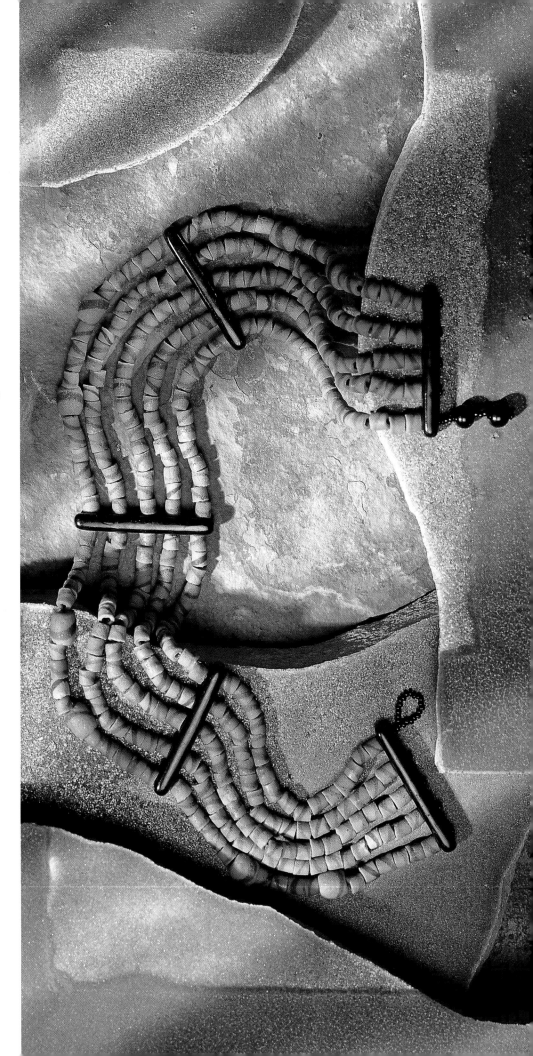

BEADED SCARF

Velvet and beads seem to have a particular affinity, as the lustrous texture of the fabric makes the two-cut rocaille beads appear even more iridescent and shimmery.

YOU WILL NEED
•

Beads and findings
- 1 × 30mm blue disk
- ⅛ ounce gold rocaille beads, size 12/0
- ¼ ounce two-cut purple rocaille beads
- 34 × 4mm gold beads
- 3 × 10mm red beads
- 4 × 4mm red disks
- 6 × 8mm blue beads
- 4 small pearl drops (approximately 6 × 10mm)
- 2 large crystal drops (approximately 10 × 15mm)
- 3 × 8mm pearl beads
- 2 × 14mm red disks
- 3 large purple drops (approximately 15 × 22mm)
- Beading thread
- Beading needle

Other equipment
- Scarf, approximately 11½ inches wide
- Dressmaker's pins
- Scissors

MAKING THE CENTRAL DROP

1 Use a pin to mark the middle of the scarf. Place two pins on either side of the central pin at evenly spaced points. These points should be about 2¼ inches apart.

2 Take a length of beading thread through the middle of the large blue disk, leaving a 3 inch tail, and pick up approximately 25 gold rocailles. Take the thread back through the large disk.

3 Continue adding rows of 25 gold rocailles, for a total of 10 rows, arranging them around the outside of the large disk. Finish off.

4 Attach a length of thread firmly to the wrong side of the middle of the scarf and pick up 12 purple rocailles, one 4mm gold bead, three purple rocailles, one 4mm gold bead, one 10mm red bead, and one 4mm gold bead.

5 Take the thread through an edge bead in one of the rows of gold rocailles around the large blue disk, then take the thread back through all the beads just picked up and work a firm overstitch at the edge.

6 Bring out the thread about ½ inch to one side of the central point and pick up four purple rocailles, one gold bead, and 13 purple rocailles. Take the thread through the gold, red, and gold beads, then back through the beads you have just picked up. Work a firm overstitch at the edge.

7 Bring out the thread about ½ inch farther along the edge of the scarf and pick up 15 purple rocailles, one 4mm gold bead, and six purple rocailles. Take the thread through the gold, red, and gold beads again, then back through the beads you have just picked up. Work one or two firm overstitches and finish off the thread.

8 Repeat steps 6 and 7 twice more on the other side of the drop.

FINISHING THE CENTRAL DROP

1 Find the bottom central row of gold rocailles on the large blue disk and attach a length of thread to a rocaille along the edge. Pick up five purple rocailles, one pearl bead, one gold bead, one large purple drop, and three gold rocailles. Miss the gold rocailles and take the thread back through the beads just picked up, then take it through the gold rocailles at the center of the blue disk and bring it back through the next row of gold rocailles, bringing the thread through on the edge of the disk.

2 Pick up seven purple rocailles, one gold bead, one blue bead, and three gold rocailles. Miss the gold rocailles and take the thread back through the beads you have just picked up and back up through the gold rocailles around the blue disk.

3 Work the thread down through the strand of gold rocailles on the other side of the center and repeat step 2 to add another matching drop. ▶

Wooden beads add interest to a plain chiffon scarf.

▶ MAKING THE INTERNAL DROPS

1 Attach the thread to a point near one of the marking pins. You are going to attach seven individual drops, the first and last of which should align with the marking pins, with the other five spaced evenly between them.

2 Pick up four purple rocailles, one 4mm gold bead, one small red disk, and three gold rocailles. Miss the three gold rocailles and take the thread back through the red disk, the gold bead, and the purple rocailles. Make a firm overstitch at the edge of the scarf.

3 Bring the thread out about ½ inch along the edge, pick up eight purple rocailles, one gold bead, one 8mm blue bead, and three gold rocailles. Miss the gold rocailles and take the thread back through the other beads. Make a firm overstitch at the edge of the scarf.

4 Bring the thread out about ½ inch along the edge, pick up 13 purple rocailles, one gold bead, one pearl drop, and three gold rocailles. Miss the gold rocailles and take the thread back through the other beads. Make a firm overstitch at the edge of the scarf.

5 Bring the thread out about ½ inch along the edge, pick up six purple rocailles, one gold bead, one 10mm red bead, one gold bead, six purple rocailles, one gold bead, one crystal drop, and three gold rocailles. Miss the gold rocailles and take the thread back through the other beads. Make a firm overstitch at the edge of the scarf.

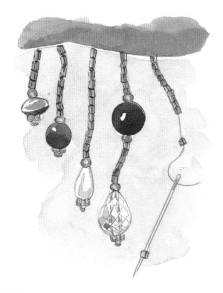

6 Repeat steps 4, 3, and 2 to make the group of seven drops symmetrical.

7 Repeat steps 1–6 on the other side.

MAKING THE END DROPS

1 Attach the thread about 1 inch from one end of the scarf and pick up five purple rocailles, one gold bead, five purple rocailles, one pearl bead, one gold bead, one 14mm red disk, one gold bead, one large purple drop, and three gold rocailles. Miss the gold rocailles and take the thread back through the other beads. Make a firm overstitch at the edge of the scarf.

2 Bring the thread out about ½ inch from the drop just sewn and pick up 15 purple rocailles. Take the thread through the rocaille above the pearl bead on the drop and back through the rocailles.

3 Repeat step 2 to add two symmetrical strands at each side of the drop. The two outside strands should have 16 purple rocailles.

4 Repeat steps 1–3 at the other end of the scarf.

GARLAND NECKLACE

This necklace conjures up pictures of the garlands draped around Christmas trees, but it's pretty enough to wear around your neck. Matching earrings add a festive touch.

YOU WILL NEED
•

Beads and findings
- 1 × 10mm black bead
- ¼ ounce black rocaille beads, size 8/0
- ½ ounce black bugles
- 1 ounce mixed rocaille beads, size 12/0
- 20 × 14mm black beads
- Beading needle
- Beading thread

Other equipment
- Scissors

MAKING THE NECKLACE

1 For the loop, take a long piece of thread and pick up one black rocaille and 28 red rocailles, leaving a 3 inch tail. Take the thread back through the black rocaille, forming a loop.

2 Pick up one bugle, one 8/0 rocaille, continuing in this way until there are six rocailles and seven bugles.

3 Pick up a 12/0 rocaille and a 14mm bead. Pick up 12 12/0 rocailles of one color and go back through the large bead. Repeat four times. Pick up a 12/0 rocaille.

4 Repeat step 2, then repeat step 3 using a different color rocaille. Continue for a total of six 14mm beads with rocailles separated by seven bugle groups.

5 Form the clasp by picking up the 10mm black bead and nine purple 12/0 rocailles. Take the thread back through the 10mm bead. Repeat for nine rows of rocailles. Finish off.

6 Starting at the loop end, attach a new length of thread. Take it back through the first 8/0 rocaille, on the first strand, then pick up one bugle, one 8/0 rocaille, and one bugle. Repeat step 3.

7 Continue this strand for a total of seven 14mm beads with rocailles, separated by six groups of bugles. End with five bugles alternated with four 8/0 rocailles, then attach the thread to the black bead that forms the clasp.

8 Repeat steps 6 and 7, but starting at the opposite side.

FRINGED LAMPSHADE

The design of this cheerful bead-fringed lamp was inspired by Victorian antiques. It looks equally good either suspended from the ceiling or used with decorative stands.

YOU WILL NEED

•

Beads and findings
- 1½ ounces red rocaille beads, size 12/0
- 42 × 27mm silver bugles
- 42 × 8mm red beads
- Beading thread
- Beading needle

Other equipment
- Approximately 16 inches bias binding (we used white)
- Approximately 16 inches decorative braid
- Small lampshade, approximately 4½ inches in diameter
- Ruler or tape measure
- Pencil
- Scissors
- Clear, all-purpose glue
- Tissue paper, clothespins, or masking tape

MAKING THE DROPS

1 Check that the bias binding and braid fit around the edge of the shade, then make 42 evenly spaced marks along the center of the binding, fold the binding in half lengthwise (so that the short ends are inside) and hold it together with a few drops of glue.

2 Tie a knot in one end of a long piece of thread and attach it to the binding.

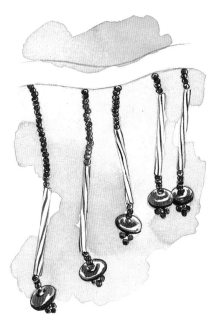

3 Pick up four rocailles, one bugle, four rocailles, one 8mm bead, and four rocailles. Miss the last bead and take the thread up through all the other beads. Take the thread to the back of the bias binding and bring your needle out at the next penciled mark.

4 Repeat step 3.

5 Make the next drop by picking up 10 rocailles, one bugle, four rocailles, one 8mm bead, and four rocailles. Miss the last bead and take the thread back up through all the other beads. Take the thread to the back of the bias binding and bring your needle out at the next penciled mark.

6 Make the next drop by picking up 16 rocailles, one bugle, four rocailles, one 8mm bead, and four rocailles. Miss the last bead and take the thread back up through all the other beads. Take the thread to the back of the bias binding and bring your needle out at the next penciled mark.

7 Make the longest drop in the pattern by picking up 22 rocailles, one bugle, four rocailles, one 8mm bead, and four rocailles. Miss the last bead and take the thread up through all the other beads. Take the thread to the back of the bias binding and bring your needle out at the next penciled mark.

You could simplify the pattern by making the strands the same length.

8 Repeat step 6 (with 16 rocailles at the top), then repeat step 5 (with 10 rocailles at the top).

9 Repeat step 3 twice.

10 Continue in this way until you have 42 drops. You should end with step 5 (ie, with 10 rocailles at the top) and you should have a total of six long drops (ie, with 22 rocailles at the top).

ATTACHING THE TRIMMING

1 Trim the bias binding so that it fits neatly around the outside of the lampshade and so that the distance between the first and last drop is the same as the distance between all the other drops. The ends of the bias binding should not overlap.

2 Apply a line of glue around the outside edge of the lampshade, allow the glue to become tacky and apply the binding. You may need to support the beads on some crumpled tissue paper so that their weight does not pull the binding out of place. Alternatively, use clothespins or masking tape to hold the binding in place until the glue is dry.

3 Apply a line of glue around the outside edge on top of the binding and glue the decorative braid in position, fitting the ends neatly together.

WIREWORK

Once you have mastered some basic wirework techniques, you will have the skills to accomplish many other aspects of jewelry making.

The most important aspect of wirework is practice, but the results are very rewarding. As well as the projects that follow, you could decorate chains with something dangling from every link or you could hang wired beads from simple hoop earrings. You can also practice more skills with your wire and make neat wound tops to hang a bead sideways or suspend a semiprecious disk.

Fig. 1

Fig. 2

TYPES OF WIRE The most readily available wires for wirework are head pins and eye pins, sold mainly for earring making, but easy to adapt for other uses. Head pins have a flat end and fit snugly against the end of a bead, while eye pins have a neat loop at one end, which is useful for joining several beads. You can also buy rolls of wire, available mainly in plated copper, in a variety of thicknesses (from 0.4–1.2) and finishes, such as silver and brass. Wood, plastic, or lightweight glass beads will be fine on head or eye pins, but as the beads get heavier you will want something more substantial — 0.8 wire is a good gauge to use.

EQUIPMENT You will need round-nosed pliers for wirework. A small pair is good for delicate work and a larger pair can be used for bigger loops and chunkier effects. Try to avoid pliers with very long points as these can make your work seem very remote from your control. Wire cutters are also useful. A small file can be used to smooth any rough edges on the wire.

TURNING Before you make any of the projects it is a good idea to practice turning loops with

some spare eye pins or wire. Rest the bottom of your eye pin on the third finger of your left hand. Hold the top with your left thumb and index finger. Holding your pliers in your right hand, bend the top ¼ inch of the wire toward you (*fig. 1*). (Left-handers will need to reverse these instructions.) If you are using thicker wire you will need more of it and you should work with larger pliers – practice with different effects. When the top of the wire is facing toward you at a 45° angle, move your pliers to the top of the wire and roll the eye pin away from you, bending the wire around the top of your pliers as you move it. You can take the pliers out and repeat (*fig. 2*) until the wire has a neat loop at the top. Make sure there isn't a gap between the loop and the straight piece of wire. When turning a loop at both ends of a bead, be sure they are both facing the same way. Always remember that when you are joining loops, opening jump rings, or adding ear wires, you must open your loops sideways so that you keep the neat, round shape.

1 *Jump rings*
2 *Eye pins and head pins*
3 *Wire cutters*
4 *Round-nosed pliers*
5 *Copper wire*
6 *Gold wire*
7 *Silver wire*

NOVELTY EARRINGS

We attached an assortment of beads to lengths of link chain and the result is an abundance of earrings in a riot of colors. You can make the earrings as long or as short as you like.

YOU WILL NEED

•

Beads and findings
- 2 lengths of large-link chain, each about 1¼ inches per pair
- Long drop beads
- Rocaille beads, size 12/0
- About 14 assorted beads per pair
- Large jump rings
- Eye pins and head pins
- Earring hooks

Other equipment
- Flat-nosed pliers
- Round-nosed pliers
- Scissors
- Wire cutters

WIRING THE BEADS

1 Use flat-nosed pliers to open a jump ring sideways.
2 Attach a bead to the jump ring and close up. Repeat for the second earring.

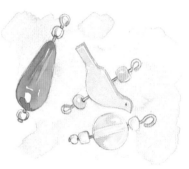

3 Continue threading a mix of rocailles and larger beads onto jump rings, eye pins, or head pins as your design dictates. Trim, leaving enough for a loop, and turn a loop with round-nosed pliers (see pages 42–43). For a 1¼ inch length of chain, you will need 6–8 wired bead groupings per earring.

MAKING THE EARRINGS

1 Attach a feature bead to one end of a length of chain.
2 Open the loops in the wired beads you have just made, using flat-nosed pliers to open them sideways, and attach each to a link in the chain. Close the loops.

3 Continue to add bead drops to links in the chain, leaving one or two links free at the top.
4 Attach the ear hooks.

We used only one length of chain for these earrings, but several lengths could be attached to a jump ring and then to an earring finding for a fuller effect. The single chain technique could also be used to make a necklace or a charm bracelet.

Swivel Necklace

Always have extra eye pins handy when you are making necklaces like this – it is not always easy to turn a neat loop every single time.

YOU WILL NEED
•

Beads and findings
- 14 × 1 inch eye pins
- 5 × 1½ inch eye pins
- 94 × 4mm wooden beads
- 5 silver-finish beads
- 8 × 3mm silver beads
- 18 silver swivel fittings
- 2 figure-eight silver fittings
- 1 snap fastener

Other equipment
- Round-nosed pliers

MAKING THE NECKLACE

1 Make all 19 beaded links by arranging the beads on the eye pins and turning neat loops at the top. You will need 14 links of wooden beads with one magenta, one teal, one blue, one teal, and one magenta. You will need 5 links as follows: two links of one magenta, one 3mm silver, one blue, one silver-finish, one blue, one 3mm silver, one magenta; two links of one teal, one 3mm silver, one blue, one silver-finish, one blue, one 3mm silver, one teal. The central link has one magenta, one teal, one blue, one silver-finish, one blue, one teal, one magenta. The necklace shown measures 13 inches.

2 Taking one all-wooden beaded link, open the loop sideways and insert a loop of one swivel. Use your pliers to close the loop, taking care to keep it as smooth as possible. Repeat five more times. Attach one magenta-silver link, one swivel, one all-wooden link, one swivel, one teal-silver link, one swivel, then the central link.

For the earrings, thread one wooden and two silver beads onto three eye pins of different lengths and put a swivel on one end. Attach the earring hooks. The bracelet has five links of 8mm and 4mm wooden beads with silver beads, and four swivel fittings. The clasp is attached as for the necklace.

3 Repeat the pattern in step 2 to complete the necklace.

4 Use the figure-eight fittings to attach the snap fastener to the ends of the chain. Remember to open the fittings sideways. If you cannot find figure-eight fittings, make your own from two eye pins, cutting them off above the loop and bending back the end in the opposite direction to form a tight S-shape, or use large jump rings.

CHUNKY CHAIN NECKLACE

This whimsical assortment of linked beads on a chain is easy to make and easy to wear. Because the pattern is busy, keep the color scheme simple.

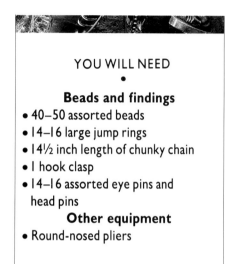

YOU WILL NEED

•

Beads and findings

- 40–50 assorted beads
- 14–16 large jump rings
- 14½ inch length of chunky chain
- 1 hook clasp
- 14–16 assorted eye pins and head pins

Other equipment

- Round-nosed pliers

MAKING THE NECKLACE

1 Make the 12 beaded links by arranging the beads on the eye pins and head pins. The central link should be the longest. Use small beads at the base of links with large-holed beads to prevent them from slipping off.

2 Lay the chain flat and experiment with the positioning of the links until you find a pattern you like. The links should not extend too far from the central point or they may fall behind your shoulders when worn.

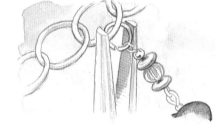

3 Start with the central beaded link. Use your pliers to open a jump ring sideways, thread on the link at the center of the chain and attach. Close up the jump ring. Repeat with the other beaded links.

4 Attach two jump rings at one end of the chain. Open another jump ring and thread on the clasp. Attach the jump ring and clasp to the other end and close.

CELESTIAL BLUES SET

A casually elegant bracelet with earrings to match, the perfect thing to dress up a weekend outfit. The finished bracelet is about 8 inches long.

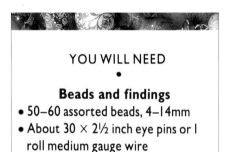

YOU WILL NEED

•

Beads and findings
- 50–60 assorted beads, 4–14mm
- About 30 × 2½ inch eye pins or 1 roll medium gauge wire
- 2 × 5-strand spacer bars
- 6 head pins
- 1 × 2-strand clasp
- 4 jump rings

Other equipment
- Wire cutters
- Round-nosed pliers

MAKING THE BRACELET

1 Wire each bead separately so that there is a loop at each end.

2 Join the beads together by opening the wire loops sideways and linking them up. Close tightly, but do not squash the wire together because this will look untidy.

3 Make five strands of linked beads, each of equal length (the strands shown here are about 6½ inches long).

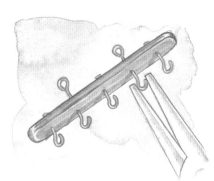

4 Thread a head pin through the central hole and two outside holes of each spacer bar, making sure that all the loops come out on the same side. Thread eye pins through the other four holes (two on each spacer bar), turning loops on the straight sides.

5 Connect the strands of beads to the loops on the spacer bars.

6 Use jump rings to connect the bracelet clasp to the loops on the spacer bars.

MAKING THE EARRINGS

1 Wire each bead separately so that there is a loop at each end. Select two identical beads for the central drop and thread a head pin through each, turning a loop at one end.

2 Thread a head pin through one of the outer holes of each spacer bar. Cut the wire to size and turn a loop.

3 Repeat step 2 with the other holes on both spacer bars, but leave the central holes free.

YOU WILL NEED

•

Beads and findings
- 36 assorted beads, 4–10mm
- 2 × 14mm beads
- 2 × 5mm beads
- 15 eye pins or 1 roll medium gauge wire
- 10 head pins
- 2 × 5-strand spacer bars
- 1 pair of earring hooks

Other equipment
- Wire cutters
- Round-nosed pliers

4 Make the drops by linking the wired beads together. You will need four strands (two for each earring), two longer than the others, so that when they are looped from the spacer bars they do not overlap.

5 Attach one of the longer strands to the outer loop on one of the spacer bars. Join one of the shorter strands to the inner loop. Repeat for the other spacer bar.

6 Thread an eye pin up through the central hole of each spacer bar. Thread one 14mm bead and one 5mm bead onto each pin. Cut the pin to length, turn a loop and connect an earring hook.

7 Connect the central drops to the lower end of the loops. Connect the two outer strands to their corresponding loops on each of the spacer bars.

When calculating the length of strands to fit your wrist, remember to include the clasp in your final measure.

CRYSTAL DROP NECKLACE

*Once you have mastered the technique of wiring beads together,
you will be astonished at the variety of pieces you can make.
Wear this crystal set for a glittering night out.*

YOU WILL NEED
•

Beads and findings
- About 23 eye pins
- 72 × 8mm crystal facet beads
- 26 × 6mm crystal facet beads
- 6 × 4mm crystal facet beads
- About 9 head pins
- 3 large teardrops with vertical holes
- 4 × ¼ inch jump rings
- 4 small teardrops with horizontal holes
- 2 calotte crimp beads
- 24 × 3mm gold beads
- I single-strand clasp
- Thick multi-filament thread
- Beading needle

Other equipment
- Round-nosed pliers
- Wire cutters

MAKING THE DROPS

I Use eye pins and turn a loop on either side of 38 8mm beads.

2 Repeat step 1 but using 24 6mm beads.

3 Use the head pins and turn a loop on six 4mm beads and the three large teardrops.

4 Thread the four jump rings through the tops of the four small teardrops.

5 Construct the drops as shown in the diagram.

MAKING THE NECKLACE

I Cut a 20 inch length of thread and knot one end. Add a calotte and squeeze it over the knot.

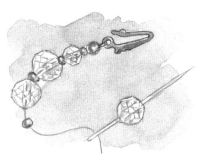

2 Thread onto the multi-filament one 3mm bead, one 6mm bead, one 3mm bead, and one 8mm bead. Then, beginning with a 3mm bead, thread 3mm and 8mm beads alternately until a total of 11 3mm and 11 8mm beads have been threaded.

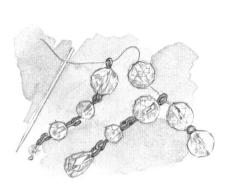

3 Take the thread through the top loop of the first drop, then pick up one 8mm bead. Continue to pick up drops in order, alternating each one with an 8mm bead, until all the drops are on the thread.

4 Pick up one 8mm bead after the last drop, then one 3mm bead. Alternate 8mm and 3mm beads until there are 11 8mm beads.

5 After the last 3mm bead, thread on one 6mm bead and another 3mm bead. Thread the other calotte onto the thread, tie a large knot in the thread so that it sits in the calotte. Tie further knots if necessary to hold the thread tight. Cut the thread and squeeze the calotte over the knot.

6 Thread the loop on the calotte through the loop on the clasp and close it. Repeat on the other side.

Each earring is made from two small teardrops with horizontal holes, one large teardrop with a horizontal hole, and one 4mm crystal facet bead.

FIVE-DROP PENDANT

Wirework lends itself particularly well to this simple-to-make pendant, which is ideal for the many beautifully shaped and colored drop beads that are available.

MAKING THE DROPS

1 Place a silver bead at the bottom of a head pin, then add a drop bead. Cut the wire to length and turn a loop with the pliers. Repeat with all the drop beads.

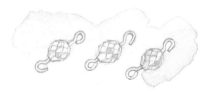

2 Take a spare length of wire, turn a loop at one end and pick up a green bead. Turn a loop at the other end of the wire. Repeat this step with all the green beads.

3 Turn a loop in one end of a length of wire and pick up one silver bead, the round, pink bead, and another silver bead. Turn a loop at the other end of the wire.

MAKING THE PENDANT

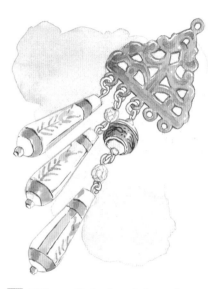

1 When all the beads have been wired, use a jump ring to connect one of the drops to the outside loop of the pendant. Open a loop sideways on one of the other drops and attach a green bead. Use a jump ring to attach this drop to one of the inner loops of the pendant. Attach a green bead to another drop, then add the round, pink bead at the top. Attach this drop to the central loop of the pendant with a jump ring.
2 Attach the remaining outer drops as in step 1.
3 Open the medium jump ring and attach it to the hole at the top of the pendant. Thread through a length of cord or leather to form the neckpiece. Knot the leather at the desired length.

Simple pendants like these are good for using up leftover or odd-numbered sets of beads.

YOU WILL NEED
•

Beads and findings
- 7 × 2.5mm silver beads
- 5 head pins
- 5 long, pink Peruvian flower drop beads
- 1 roll medium gauge wire
- 4 × 4mm green beads
- 5 small jump rings
- 1 × 10mm round, pink Peruvian bead
- 1 × 5-strand bronze pendant
- 1 medium jump ring

Other equipment
- Round-nosed pliers
- Wire cutters

DECORATIVE FLOWERS

Wire helps to keep these flowers in shape, so you can use the technique to make everlasting bouquets or corsages, or individual decorations for a table setting.

PURPLE ORCHID

MAKING THE LEAVES

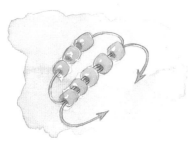

1 Cut a 20 inch length of wire. Thread on three green rocailles and push them to the center of the wire. Pick up five green rocailles with one end of wire and take the other end through these five rocailles. Pull the wire tightly.

2 Pick up seven assorted green rocailles on one end of wire and take the other end through all seven.

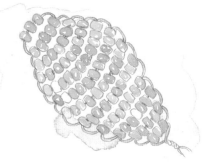

3 Continue picking up rocailles, following the diagram. Remember to pull the wire tightly after adding each row of rocailles.

4 When you have finished the pattern, twist the two ends of wire together until you have a stem of about 2 inches. Cut the wire.

5 Make four more leaves in the same way. ▶

This pink iris is made in the same way as the orchid but, instead of leaves, silver bugles, pink rocailles, and large pink oval beads were used to make five stamens, while pale pink and transparent rocailles were used for the five petals.

MAKING THE PETALS

1 Cut a 20 inch length of wire. Thread on three light purple rocailles and push them to the center of the wire. Pick up one light purple, three dark purple, and one light purple rocailles with one end of the wire and take the other end through these five rocailles. Pull tightly.

2 Pick up one light purple, four dark purple, and one light purple rocailles, and take the other end of the wire through all six rocailles. Pull the wire tightly.

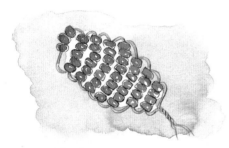

3 Continue picking up rocailles, following the illustration. When the rows are completed, twist the two wires together until you have a stem of about 2 inches. Cut the wire.

4 Make four more purple petals in the same way.

MAKING THE FLOWER

1 Take the large purple bead and thread it onto the center of a short length of wire. Twist the two ends of wire together.

2 Twist the stems of two of the petals together around the wire of the large bead. Twist the other three petals, one at a time, around the stem formed by the first two, shaping them to the form of a flower.

3 Twist the stems of the leaves, one by one, around the flower stem, arranging the leaves between but slightly below the petals.

4 When the flower is complete, take a final length of wire and, starting at the top of the stem, wrap it tightly over the other wires to make the stem tidy. Cut off any excess wires at the bottom.

RED ROSE

MAKING THE PETALS

1 Cut a 20 inch length of fine gauge wire. Thread on two red rocailles and push them to the center of the wire. Pick up four red rocailles with one end of the wire and take the other end through these four rocailles. Pull tightly.

2 Pick up six rocailles and take the other end of the wire through all six rocailles. Pull the wire tightly.

3 Continue picking up rocailles, following the illustration. When the rows are completed, twist the two wires together until you have a stem of about 2 inches. Cut the wires.

4 Make eight more petals in the same way, pressing the wire slightly so that they curve inward a little.

5 Twist the stems of three of the petals together, holding the petals upward so that they form a bud shape.

6 Attach the stems of three more petals just beneath the bud.

7 Finally, attach the last three petals so that they open slightly outward and so that they lie just below the others.

MAKING THE LEAVES

1 Cut a 20 inch length of fine gauge wire. Thread on one green rocaille and push it to the center of the wire. Pick up two more green rocailles with one end of the wire and take the other end through these two rocailles. Pull the wire tightly.

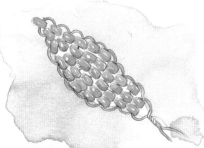

2 Continue picking up rocailles, following the illustration. Make two leaves.

MAKING THE FLOWER

1 Take the length of medium gauge wire and twist it onto the stem of the rose to make a stem about 6 inches long.

2 Take one leaf and twist on the stem about ½ inch from the bottom of the rose. Twist on the second leaf about ½ inch below the first leaf.

3 Twist a length of fine gauge wire all down the stem to give a neat finish. Cut off all the ends.

Use these flowers to add a unique touch to gift-wrappings for special occasions.

FREEHAND

AND

WEAVING
LOOMWORK

P ieces of woven work with beads bring to mind the intricacies of native American and African beadwork and the memories of Victorian beaded chokers.

EQUIPMENT You will need to use fine beading needles for freehand weaving and loomwork, which are sold in numbered sizes — the higher numbers are finer. Fine cotton thread is often supplied with bead looms, but very fine polyester thread will be stronger. You should use a thread without any "spring" in it, so unless your beads are tiny, waxed cotton or polyester or silk thread will be ideal. When you are working with small beads, you will need to be in a good light, and you will need small containers for your beads. Beware of old yogurt pots as these are too light. You can buy clear plastic stacking boxes or divided fishing trays, which are ideal. A pair of fine-pointed, curved tweezers are also a great help. It is also useful to have some extra wax on hand.

LOOMWORK You can buy metal or wooden bead looms, and the loom should be sturdy or you may have difficulty with the tension. Use strong warp (lengthwise) thread, such as the silk thread suggested in the projects. Thread the loom as shown (*fig. 1*), allowing one thread more than is required for your pattern. If you need extra strength, double up on the outside warps. For example, nine warps for a six-bead width. You should cut your warps about 20 inches longer than your planned design. When you start to bead your loom, cut about 35 inches of beading thread. Use a waxed thread, or keep it well waxed as you work, to help avoid tangles.

The positioning of the threads in the bead once they are woven on a loom is shown in *fig. 2*. When you need more thread, make sure that you knot onto your working thread and weave both strands back through the beads so that the knot will be covered.

You can plan your own designs on a grid; remember that rocailles are not completely round so your design will lengthen a little.

FREEHAND WEAVING Beads can also be woven off a loom, allowing for less geometric patterns and intricate fringe detail. Freehand weaving is generally done with rocaille beads, and a good even quality, such as Japanese rocailles, is needed.

INSTRUCTIONS FOR THREADING A LOOM Tie the required number of warp threads together with a knot at one end. Trim the threads close to the knot. Put the knot under the nail in the loom roller closest to you. Divide the warps in two halves and turn the spool until you have enough warp thread left to knot and place around the nail on the other loom roller. Turn this second roller until the warps are well tensioned over the separator bars. Use your tweezers to separate each warp into its own slot. Retension the rollers when all your warps are in position. You are now ready to attach your beading thread to the outside warp and begin your project.

1 Opaque rocailles
2 Transparent rocailles
3 Beading loom
4 Warp threads
5 Beading wax

Fig. 1

Fig. 2

SAPPHIRE CHOKER

We used pale sapphire-colored faceted beads to make this turn-of-the-century-style choker, which will add timeless elegance to any modern outfit.

YOU WILL NEED
•

Beads and findings
- 138 × 8mm sapphire faceted beads
- ⅛ ounce rocaille beads, size 12/0
- Waxed beading thread
- Beading needle

Other equipment
- Scissors

This technique is successful with a variety of different bead shapes and colors. Once you have mastered it, try making other pieces: watchstraps, bracelets, and even shorter lengths to dangle from earring hooks.

MAKING THE CHOKER

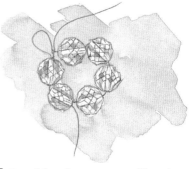

1 Double a long piece of beading thread. Pick up six beads, tie them in a circle, leaving a 6 inch tail, and pass the thread back through two beads.

2 Pick up five beads, miss one bead on the first circle, and take the thread up through the next bead.

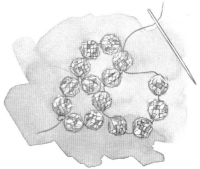

3 Pick up four beads, miss one bead on the second circle, and take the thread down through the next bead.

4 Repeat step 3, picking up four beads, until there are three beads left.

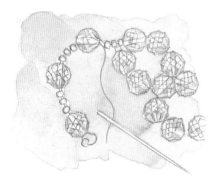

5 When you have completed the final sequence of four, run the thread back through two of the beads. Pick up three rocailles, one bead, three rocailles, one bead, three rocailles, one bead, and one rocaille. Miss the last rocaille and run the thread back to the first rocaille threaded. Instead of running the thread through this rocaille, pick up another rocaille and run the thread through the bead next to the one through which the thread originally emerged. Finish off.

6 Use the tail at the other end to pick up approximately 19 rocailles. Take the thread back through the second rocaille, pick up another rocaille, and run the thread through the bead next to the one through which the tail of the thread originally emerged. Finish off the thread.

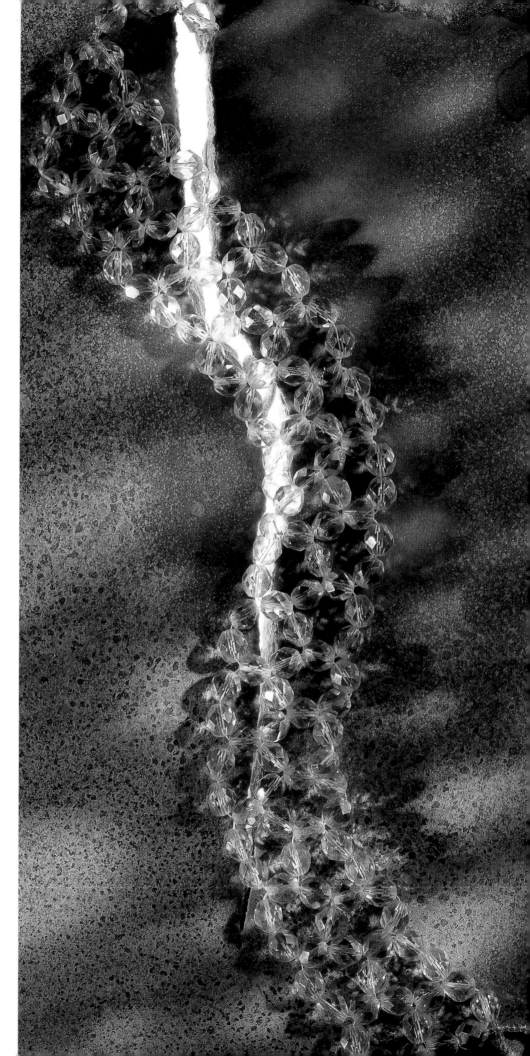

RHINESTONE & PEARL NECKLACE

This elegant necklace is the perfect classic accessory. The rhinestone spacer bars provide just the necessary sparkle, while the matching bracelet is kept plain.

YOU WILL NEED
•
Beads and findings
- 101 × 8mm pearl beads
- 4 × 3mm silver beads
- 1 × 2-strand rhinestone clasp
- 2 × 2-strand rhinestone spacer bars
- 2 beading needles
- Beading thread
Other equipment
- Scissors

MAKING THE NECKLACE

1 Take two pieces of thread, about 27 inches each, one on each needle. The finished length of the necklace is about 15 inches, not including the clasp.

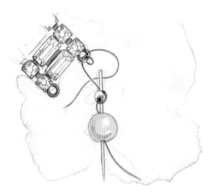

2 Use one piece of thread to pick up one pearl bead and one silver bead, leaving a 3 inch tail. Sew twice around one loop on the clasp and take the thread back down through the silver and pearl beads.

3 Repeat step 2, but using the other length of thread and sewing around the other clasp on the loop.

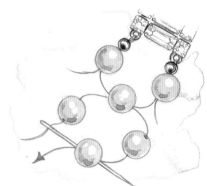

4 Working from the top to the bottom, begin weaving by using the thread on the left to pick up one pearl bead. Take the thread on the right through this bead. Pull tightly.

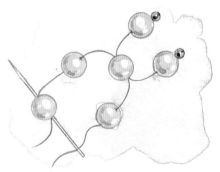

5 Use the thread on the left to pick up two pearl beads. Use the thread on the right to pick up one pearl bead and take the thread through the bead that is also on the left-hand thread. Pull tightly.

6 Repeat step 5 twice more. (You will have strung a total of 12 pearl beads).

Make the matching bracelet in exactly the same way, using smaller pearl beads and omitting the spacer bars.

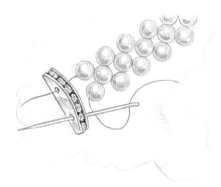

7 Use the left-hand thread to pick up one pearl bead, then take the thread through the hole in the rhinestone spacer. Repeat with the right-hand thread.

8 Use the left-hand thread to pick up two pearl beads. Use the thread on the right to pick up one pearl bead and take the thread through one of the beads on the left-hand thread (see step 4).

9 Repeat step 8 22 times (for a total of 71 pearls after the spacer bar). Add the other rhinestone spacer bar as shown in step 7.

10 Repeat step 8 four times. Use the left-hand thread to pick up one pearl bead and one silver bead. Sew twice around one loop on the clasp and pull tightly. Repeat with the right-hand thread.

11 Take the right-hand thread through the central pearl bead so that both threads meet. Tie them together and finish off securely. Repeat with the threads at the other end.

SHOE CLIPS

Extend your wardrobe by making these simple decorations to attach to plain shoes. Facet beads give that extra bit of sparkle and sophistication.

MAKING THE CLIPS

1 Find 14 bugles that are the same length (they tend to vary in size) and lay them side by side on your work surface.

2 Take a long length of beading thread and pick up two bugles, leaving a 3 inch tail.

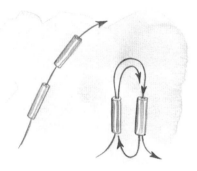

3 Take the thread back up the first bugle, forming a circle, then pull it tight so that the bugles sit firmly side by side. Take the thread back down the second bugle.

4 Pick up another bugle, take the thread back down the second bugle, pull it tight and thread it back up through the third bugle. Repeat until you have threaded all 14 bugles in this way.

YOU WILL NEED
•

Beads and findings
- ¼ ounce 9mm silver bugles
- ¼ ounce black rocaille beads, size 12/0
- ¼ ounce silver rocaille beads, size 12/0
- 5 × 6mm black facet beads
- 6 × 4mm black facet beads
- Pair of shoe clips
- Waxed beading thread
- Beading needle

Other equipment
- Scissors
- Clear, all-purpose glue

5 Pick up one black rocaille. Take the needle under the thread between two bugles and back through the rocaille. Continue until you have picked up 13 black rocailles.

6 Continuing to take the needle under the thread between beads on the previous row, pick up one black rocaille, four silver rocailles, two black rocailles, four silver rocailles and one black rocaille, giving a total of 12 rocailles.

7 Follow the illustration to add black and silver rocailles, so that there is one fewer bead on each row, until you have one black rocaille. Do not cut the thread.

MAKING THE DROPS

1 Pick up six black rocailles, one bugle, two black rocailles, one silver rocaille, one 6mm black facet bead, one silver rocaille, and three black rocailles. Miss the last three rocailles and take the thread back through all the beads and through the last bead of the triangle.

2 Take the thread through two rocailles and bring it out through the side rocaille on the third to last row of the triangle.

3 Make a drop in the same way as step 1, but use a 4mm black facet bead and only one black rocaille at the bottom, instead of three.

4 Continue in this way, adding drops to alternate side beads and alternating the drops made with 6mm facet beads (and three rocailles) and 4mm facet beads (and one rocaille).

5 When you have added the drops to both sides of the triangle, knot the thread tightly and finish off by threading it through several beads before cutting the ends.

6 Glue the shoe clip to the back of the triangle.

Another pair is made with black bugles and rocailles, 4mm black facet beads and green rocailles, and green glass disk beads.

BRICKSTITCH WATCHSTRAP

Brickstitch is a simple technique, used here to make a watchstrap in gold and dark green. But there's no limit – make a different colored strap for each day of the week!

MAKING THE STRAP

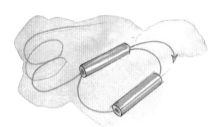

1 Pick up one gold bugle on a long piece of thread and leave a tail of about 6 inches. Pick up a green bugle. Take the thread back up through the gold bugle, forming a circle, then pull it tight so that the bugles sit firmly side by side. Take the thread back down the first green bugle picked up.

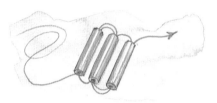

2 Pick up another gold bugle, take the thread back down the green bugle, pull it tight and thread it back up through the gold bugle.

3 Repeat, alternating green and gold bugles, until you have threaded on 11 bugles in this way, starting and ending the series with a gold bugle.

4 For the next row, pick up a gold bugle and take your needle under the thread between the last gold and green bugles on the previous row. Take the thread back up through the gold bugle. Pick up a green bugle and repeat.

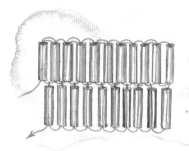

5 Continue to work in this way across the row, alternating gold and green bugles until you have three gold and two green bugles. Work to the end, but pick up a gold bugle next, until there are 10 bugles across the row. Because every row begins and ends with a gold bugle, rows with even numbers of beads will have either two gold or two green bugles in the middle.

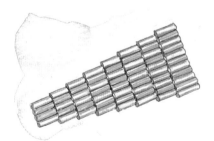

6 Continue to work rows of bugles, decreasing by one bead on each row, until you have a row of four bugles (for a total of 8 rows). Do not cut off the thread.

YOU WILL NEED
•

Beads and findings
- ¼ ounce 6mm gold bugles
- ¼ ounce 6mm dark green bugles
- ⅛ ounce gold rocaille beads, size 12/0
- 2 × 8mm gold beads
- Waxed beading thread
- Beading needle

Other equipment
- Scissors
- Watch face

This watchstrap will fit a wrist that measures 6 inches.

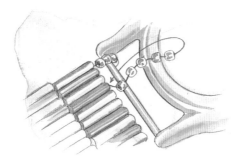

7 Bring the thread out of one of the central green bugles, pick up three rocailles, one 8mm gold bead, three rocailles, one 8mm gold bead, and one rocaille. Miss the last rocaille and take the thread back through the gold bead, the three rocailles, and the other gold bead, then through two rocailles. Pick up one rocaille and take the thread through the other green bugle in the middle. Finish off securely.

8 Using the tail left when you began, add a row of 10 bugles as in steps 4 and 5. Pick up five rocailles, take these around the bar on the watch face and take the thread back up through the last bugle.

9 Miss two bugles, pick up five rocailles and take these around the bar, then take the thread through the last bugle, as in step 8. Repeat two more times so that rocaille loops are formed from both of the end bugles and from the fourth and seventh bugles in the row. Finish off the thread securely.

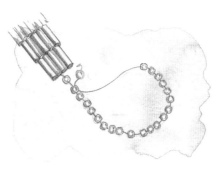

10 Work the other side of the strap to match as far as the end of step 6. Bring the working thread out through one of the central green bugles and pick up 21 rocailles. Form a loop by taking the thread through the second rocaille, pick up another rocaille and take the thread back through the other central green bugle. Finish off securely.

11 Complete the strap by attaching it to the watch face as described in steps 8 and 9.

YOU WILL NEED
•

Beads and findings
- 1½ ounces white rocaille beads, size 12/0
- ½ ounce pink rocaille beads, size 8/0
- ⅛ ounce aqua rocaille beads, size 8/0
- 13 pink drops
- Beading thread
- Beading needle

Other equipment
- Cotton cheesecloth or net
- Sewing thread

MAKING THE COVER

1 If you are using a double layer of cheesecloth, sew two circles together so that the finished diameter is approximately 4½ inches. Make a row of small running stitches around the edge.

2 Take a long length of beading thread and tie a small knot at one end. Oversew the thread at the edge of the wrong side of the fabric.

PITCHER COVERS

*These pretty covers are traditionally used to protect the milk
when having tea outdoors. Or, make a houseguest feel welcome
by covering a pitcher of water in his or her room.*

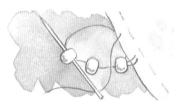

3 Pick up a white bead, take the thread through the fabric and back through the bead.

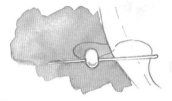

4 Pick up two white beads, go into the fabric and back up the second bead.

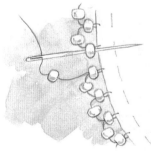

5 Repeat step 4 all around the circle of fabric. When you reach the first bead, pick up one bead and take the thread down the first bead.

6 Take the thread through one of the beads in the outer row and pick up five white, one pink, five white, one pink, five white, one pink, five white, one pink, five white, one pink, three white, one aqua, one drop, one aqua, and three white beads. Miss the last three white beads and take the thread back through the drop and the last five beads, coming out after the last pink bead.

7 Pick up five white, one pink, and five white beads and take the thread through a pink bead on the previous row (the third from the fabric).

8 Repeat step 7, taking the thread through the pink bead closest to the fabric.

9 Pick up five white beads, miss two of the white beads on the edge of the fabric and take the thread through the next white bead.

10 Pick up five white, one pink, and five white beads and take the thread through the second pink bead on the previous row.

11 Repeat step 10.

12 Pick up five white, one aqua, five white, one pink, and five white beads and take the thread through the next free pink bead on the previous row.

13 Continue all around the fabric. There should be three drops with an aqua loop between each large drop.

14 When you reach the beginning, finish off securely.

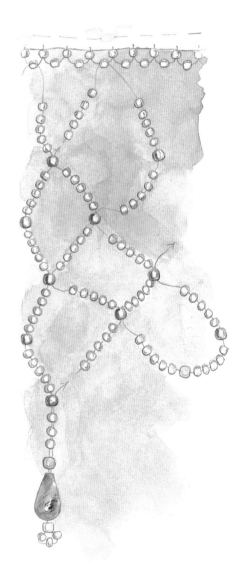

FRINGED NECKLACE

Necklaces made in this way are well suited to textured beads in natural colors, such as the turquoise and orange beads used here. The finished necklace is about 15 inches long.

YOU WILL NEED
•

Beads and findings
- 1 barrel clasp
- ¼ ounce turquoise rocaille beads, size 8/0
- 33 turquoise disks
- 22 apricot-colored barrels, approximately 10 × 17mm
- 22 turquoise rocaille beads, size 6/0
- 33 African ground glass beads
- 11 orange beads, 15mm long
- 11 orange rocaille beads, size 6/0
- Waxed beading thread
- Beading needle
Other equipment
- Scissors

MAKING THE NECKLACE

1 Cut a 69 inch length of thread. Sew one end of the thread to the clasp, leaving a tail of about 3 inches.

2 Thread on 157 8/0 turquoise rocailles. Loop and tie the thread through the other end of the clasp to secure.

4 Miss the last three rocailles and take the thread back up through the disk, the ground glass bead, the 8/0 turquoise rocaille, the orange bead, and the first of the two 8/0 turquoise rocailles.

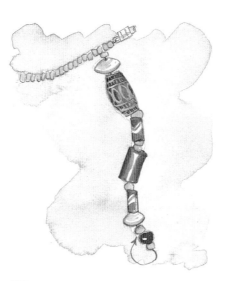

3 Take the thread back through two rocailles, pick up one 8/0 rocaille, one disk, one apricot-colored barrel, one 6/0 turquoise rocaille, one ground glass bead, two 8/0 turquoise rocailles, one long orange bead, one 8/0 turquoise rocaille, one ground glass bead, one disk, one 8/0 turquoise rocaille, one 6/0 orange rocaille, and one 8/0 turquoise rocaille.

5 Pick up one 8/0 turquoise rocaille, one ground glass bead, one 6/0 turquoise rocaille, one apricot-colored barrel, one disk, and one 8/0 turquoise rocaille.

6 Miss 13 beads on the main strand and take the thread through the next bead.

7 Repeat steps 3–5 for 10 more drops. Finish off securely.

ROSETTE EARRINGS

This is a versatile technique that takes a little patience to master — but the results are pieces of jewelry with a real professional finish.

YOU WILL NEED
•

Beads and findings
- 2 × 8mm beads
- ½ ounce rocaille beads, size 12/0
- 34 × 4mm beads
- 6 beads, approximately 10 × 17mm
- 10 × 6mm beads
- 2 jump rings
- 1 pair of earring hooks
- Waxed beading thread
- Beading needle

Other equipment
- Scissors
- Round-nosed pliers

MAKING THE ROSETTES

1 Cut 3 feet of beading thread and take it through an 8mm bead, leaving a tail of 3 inches. Take the thread around the bead, twice around one side and twice around the other side. These threads are the base for the first row.

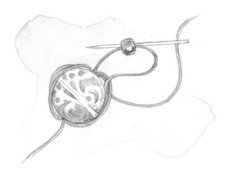

2 Pick up one rocaille on the thread. Take the thread under the threads around the bead and then back up through the rocaille.

3 Repeat this all the way around the 8mm bead until the last bead lies against the first bead. Make sure that all the rocailles are sitting evenly and that there are gaps left between them.

4 To finish the row, take the thread down through the first bead and then back up the last bead. All the rows will be finished off in this way.

5 Form the next row in the same way, but using 4mm beads. You should need about 14 beads, but do not use too many or the rosette will not lie flat. Finish as for step 4.

6 Work the next row in rocailles. Pick up one rocaille, go under the thread and back up the bead. Pick up two rocailles, go under the thread and back up, but through only one of the two beads. Continue to work in this way all around the rosette.

7 When you get to the last bead, pick up only one bead and take the thread back down through the first bead you added.

8 Finish off by running the thread back through the beads to the tail. Tie the tail and the working end together and run each through three beads before cutting off.

MAKING THE DROPS

1 Hold the rosette so that the hole in the central bead is vertical. On the outside row, one of the projecting beads should appear immediately above the vertical hole – this will form the central point for the drops.

2 Take another length of thread through two beads close to the outer edge, then through the bead to the left of the central bead. Leave a tail of 3 inches. When you begin to form the first drop, the needle will be pointing toward the central bead.

3 Pick up one rocaille, one 4mm bead, one rocaille, one 10 × 17mm bead, one rocaille, one 6mm bead, and three rocailles. Miss the last three rocailles, then take the thread back up through all the beads on the drop.

4 Go back to the protruding bead, working in the direction of the central bead. Pick up one rocaille, then take the thread through the central protruding bead. Pick up two rocailles, one 4mm bead, one rocaille, one 6mm bead, two rocailles, one 10 × 17mm bead, two rocailles, one 6mm bead, and three rocailles.

5 Finish the middle drop as the first one, then make the third drop to match the first. Finish off by tying the working thread to the tail, then threading each through three beads before cutting off.

FINISHING

1 Open one of the jump rings sideways with round-nosed pliers. Thread it through the top, central bead and through one of the earring hooks, then close it tightly.

ROSETTE NECKLACE

Beads are used to make the simple loop fastening for this necklace. Not only is the clasp attractive, but it allows for an adjustable fit.

YOU WILL NEED
•

Beads and findings
- 8 × 12mm beads
- ½ ounce rocaille beads, size 8/0
- ½ ounce two-cut rocaille beads
- ½ ounce rocaille beads, size 12/0
- 11 × 10mm beads
- 2 oval beads, approximately 11 × 18mm
- 3 teardrops, approximately 11 × 19mm
- Waxed beading thread
- Beading needle

Other equipment
- Scissors

2 Pick up one 8/0 rocaille on the thread. Take the thread under the threads around the bead and then back up through the rocaille.

3 Repeat this all the way around the central bead until the last bead lies against the first bead. Make sure that all the rocailles are sitting evenly and that there are gaps left between them.

4 Take the thread down through the first rocaille and then back up the last bead. All the rows will be finished off in this way.

7 To attach the last row, pick up one 12/0 rocaille, go under the thread, then back up the bead. Pick up two 12/0 rocailles, go under the thread, then back up the second bead only. Continue in this way around the circle. When you get to the first bead again, pick up only one bead and take the thread down through the first bead.

8 Finish off by taking the thread down through the beads, back to the tail. Tie the tail thread to the working thread, but before cutting the ends run both threads back through three beads each. Cut the thread.

9 Make eight more rosettes. You will need three more made with a central bead of 12mm and five with a central bead of 10mm. ▶

MAKING THE ROSETTES

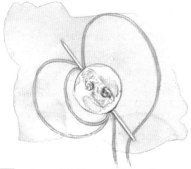

1 Thread 3 feet of thread on a beading needle, then pick up one 12mm bead, leaving a tail of 3 inches. Take the thread around the bead, twice around one side and twice around the other side. These threads are the base on which the first row of beads is worked.

5 Make a second row of rocailles in the same way. This row will be larger than the first and you will use more beads. However, take care not to use too many beads or they will not sit flat.

6 Attach a third row, this time using two-cut rocailles.

Each earring is made from one rosette with a 12mm central bead. The surrounding three rows are a single row each of 8/0 rocailles, two-cut rocailles and an outer row of 12/0 rocailles. A drop bead is added for the finishing touch.

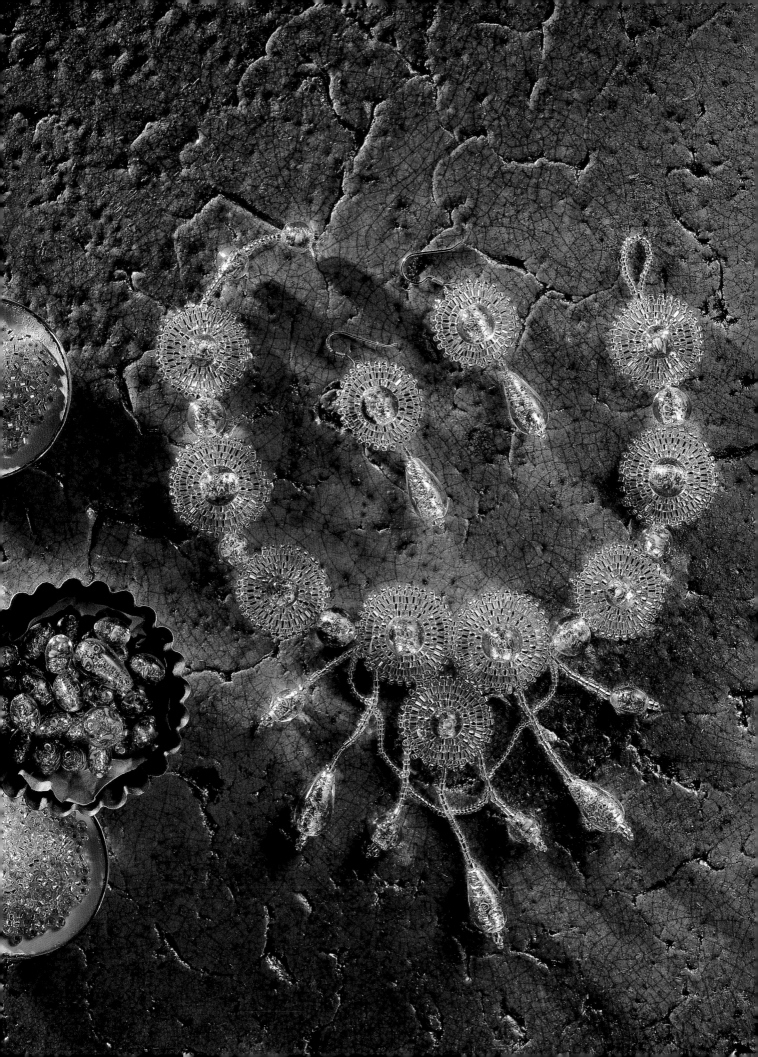

MAKING THE NECKLACE

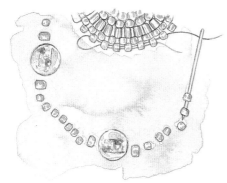

1 Take a new length of thread and bring it out through one of the outer beads in a 10mm rosette. Remember that the central bead should be vertical. Leave a tail and run the thread through a few beads. Miss the last bead, then run the thread back through the beads. Thread on approximately eight rocailles, then one 10mm bead, approximately eight rocailles, one more 10mm bead, one 8/0 rocaille, and one 12/0 rocaille. Miss the last bead and run the thread back through, finishing it off securely with the tail.

2 Take the thread through the beads on the opposite side of the rosette and attach it securely. Pick up a 12mm bead, then take the thread through the outer beads on a 12mm rosette, with the central bead positioned vertically, finishing off the thread securely as before. Continue linking rosettes, picking up a 10mm bead, a 10mm rosette (positioned vertically) and another 12mm bead.

3 Make the fastening loop at the other end of the necklace. Bring out the thread on the edge of a 10mm rosette, add one 8/0 rocaille then make the loop from 12/0 rocailles. Take the thread back through the 8/0 rocaille and back through the edge beads to finish it off with the tail. Repeat step 2.

4 The triangular centerpiece is formed by positioning two 12mm rosettes with a 10mm rosette centrally below. Before sewing, make sure that all the central beads are vertical. They are joined by their outer edges so that the beads slot together. Join the two 12mm rosettes by taking the thread through nine beads, five from one rosette and four from the other.

5 Join the lower rosette by taking about five beads from each of the larger rosettes.

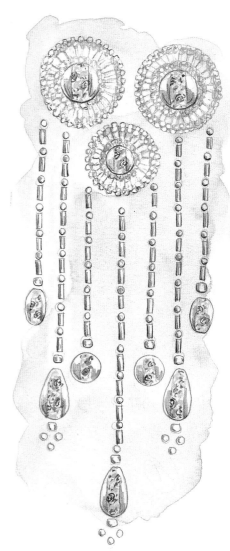

6 Complete and attach all seven drops as shown.

7 To link the drops, begin at the top of the first drop and pick up 15 12/0 rocailles. Bring this strand through the third two-cut rocaille on the next drop. Pick up 17 12/0 rocailles and go through the third two-cut rocaille on the next drop.

8 Pick up 11 12/0 rocailles and go through the fourth two-cut rocaille on the central drop. Pick up 11 rocailles and go through the third two-cut rocaille on the next drop.

9 Repeat step 7 in reverse, then finish off. Attach the central section to the side sections.

ROSETTE PENDANT

We chose subtle shades of bronze and gunmetal gray for this pendant, which looks coolly sophisticated, but it would look just as effective in pearly white.

YOU WILL NEED
•

Beads and findings
- 2 × 8mm leopard jasper beads
- ½ ounce gunmetal rocaille beads, size 8/0
- 17 × 6mm leopard jasper beads
- ½ ounce bronze rocaille beads, size 12/0
- ½ ounce pearlized rocaille beads, size 12/0
- ½ ounce 6mm bronze bugles
- 2 × 4mm malachite beads
- 1 × 8mm malachite bead
- Black beading thread
- Beading needle

Other equipment
- Scissors

MAKING THE ROSETTES

1 Make the central rosette, following the instructions for the rosette technique, which is explained in the project on pages 72–73. The central bead should be an 8mm leopard jasper bead. Then, form a row of 8/0 gunmetal rocailles and a row of 6mm leopard jasper beads (you should use nine). The remaining rows are made as follows: 12/0 bronze rocailles, 12/0 pearlized rocailles, then 8/0 gunmetal rocailles. Complete the rosette with 12/0 bronze rocailles. Finish off the thread securely.

2 Make two small rosettes with a 6mm leopard jasper bead in the middle. The first row should be of 8/0 gunmetal rocailles, followed by 12/0 bronze rocailles. Finish off all ends securely.

MAKING THE PENDANT

1 Attach two new lengths of thread on either side of the central rosette as shown. Thread approximately 16 12/0 bronze rocailles and one 12/0 pearlized rocaille onto each side.

2 Make seven drops with the same rocailles and jasper beads used in the rosette, plus the larger malachite beads. Position the rosette so that the central bead is vertical, then attach a long, central drop directly below. Attach three drops to one side. Finish off the thread securely. Turn the pendant over, join on a new length of thread, and attach the three remaining drops.

3 Attach a new length of thread to the opposite side of a small rosette, taking it back through beads on the outer circle to hold it securely. Thread on one 12/0 pearlized rocaille, then add bronze rocailles until it measures about 31 inches. Pick up one 12/0 pearlized rocaille, then take the thread through a couple of beads on the outer edge of the other small rosette. Finish off securely.

CABOCHON BROOCH

If you use abalone as the center of this brooch, try to match the rocaille beads to the changing, shimmery colors of the shell.

YOU WILL NEED
•

Beads and findings
- 1 abalone cabochon, approximately 1½ × 1¼ inches
- ½ ounce rocaille beads, size 12/0
- 1 brooch back
- Waxed beading thread
- Beading needle

Other equipment
- 1 small piece of fine leather, approximately 2½ × 2 inches
- Clear, all-purpose glue
- Scissors

PREPARING THE CABOCHON

1 Glue the cabochon to the leather and leave to dry.
2 Tie a knot in the end of a length of thread and take it through the leather from the back, making sure that it comes through to the right side of the leather at the very edge of the cabochon.

MAKING THE EDGING

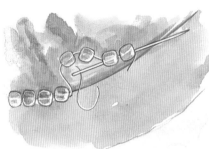

1 Pick up four rocailles. Take the needle down through the leather so that the four beads are lying against the very edge of the cabochon. Bring the needle back through to the right side, midway between the beads. Take the thread back through two of the rocailles in the direction of the work.
2 Pick up four more beads and repeat the previous step until you have worked all the way around the cabochon.

3 When you reach the end, take the thread from the last bead through the first bead, through the leather, and down to the back.

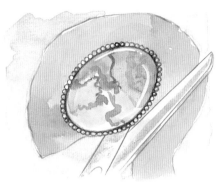

4 Trim the leather close to the edge of the first row, taking care not to cut the thread because you will continue with the working thread. You will use the edge of the leather as the basis of the next row of beads.

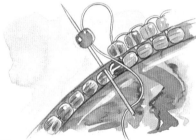

5 Pick up a bead, take your needle through the leather and back up through the bead. Repeat this all the way around the edge of the leather.

Long pearl drop beads and several gold beads can be used to add interest to an all-white brooch.

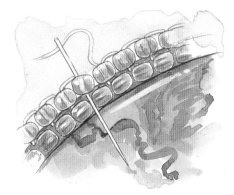

6 When you get back to the first bead, take the thread down this bead and back up the last bead. You should do this at the end of every row; the thread will continue.

7 Start the next row by using the thread between beads on the preceding row. Pick up a bead, go under the thread and back up the bead. Repeat this all the way around, making sure that the beads sit snugly together and there are no gaps between them.

8 Repeat step 7 until you have completed three more rows.

9 Form the last row by picking up one new bead. Go under the thread, back through the bead, then pick up two beads. Go under the thread, then back up the second bead. Repeat, using two beads, all the way around.

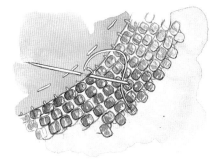

10 When you have reached the last bead, pick up one bead and go down the first bead. Run the thread back down to the leather. Over-stitch several times through the leather and cut the thread.

11 Attach a brooch back.

FLAT PEYOTE BRACELET

Gold-colored rocailles have been used to give this pretty bracelet a sophisticated touch, while the dark blue rocailles have a lovely metallic sheen.

MAKING THE BRACELET

1 Thread 12 blue beads on a long piece of thread, leaving a tail of about 3 inches.

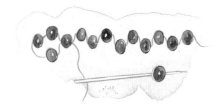

2 Pick up one blue bead, miss the first bead and take the thread through the second bead. Pick up another blue bead, miss one bead and take the thread through the next bead. Continue until you have added six new beads.

3 Tie the tail and working thread together, but do not cut the thread.

4 Pick up a blue bead, take the thread through the next protruding blue bead on the previous row and pick up a blue bead. Continue in this way to the end of the row.

5 Make 4–5 rows of solid blue rocailles, then begin working in the flower pattern. Use gold beads for the petals and red ones for the centers. We made 14 flowers.

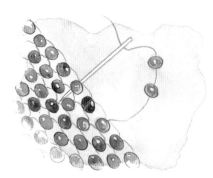

6 To make a flower at the edge, start at the beginning of a new row and pick up one gold bead, then complete the row with blue beads as before. Work the next row with blue beads, but pick up a gold bead before you take the thread through the gold bead in the previous row. Pick up a red bead on the next row and finish with blue beads. Begin the next row with blue beads, but pick up a gold bead before you take the thread through the red bead. Pick up another gold bead, then complete the row with blue beads.

7 Begin the next row with blue beads, take the thread up through the last gold bead and pick up two gold beads. Take the thread down the first two gold beads, then back up the last two gold beads.

8 Begin measuring for fit when you have woven about 6 inches. When you have reached a length that suits your wrist, work the thread to the center bead for the clasp. Pick up two blue beads, one 8mm bead, four blue beads, one 8mm bead, and one blue bead. Miss the last bead and take the thread back through the other beads before finishing it off securely.

9 Thread the tail left at the other end onto your needle and work it back to the center. Pick up enough blue beads to make a loop that will go over the 8mm red bead at the other end. Take the end back through several beads to finish off.

Another bracelet uses bronze-colored rocailles with a contrasting edging of green. The red edge flowers are made in the same way as the edge flowers in the blue bracelet. Both bracelets measure about 5½ inches, without the clasp.

Festive napkin rings

We have used silver, red, and green rocailles for these napkin rings, which makes them especially Christmassy. Although they look delicate, the rings are surprisingly robust.

MAKING THE FLAT RING

1 Leaving a tail of about 3 inches, pick up 14 silver beads on a long piece of thread.

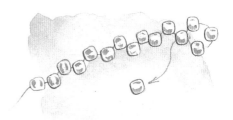

2 To begin weaving, pick up one silver bead, miss a bead and take the thread through the next bead. Pick up a silver bead, miss the next bead and take the thread through the next bead. Continue in this way to the end of the row.

3 Tie the working thread and the tail together but do not cut the thread.

The same colors – silver, red, and green – have been woven together to create a completely different effect. Why not make one to fit around the base of a candle?

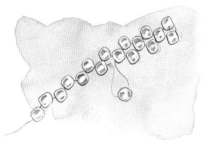

4 Pick up one silver bead and take the thread through the next protruding bead from the previous row. Repeat to the end of the row.

5 After several rows of silver, begin the pattern. (See illustration on page 82.)

6 Continue working the pattern in step 5 in reverse until the diamond is complete. Allow several rows of silver between each diamond.

2 Pick up a red bead, take the thread through the first red bead. Pick up a green bead and take the thread through the first green bead. Pick up a silver bead and take the thread through the first silver bead.

3 Take the thread back through the second red bead (the first red bead on the second row) so that the needle is in the correct position.

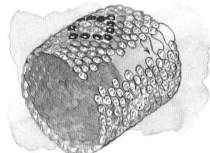

7 When the three diamonds are complete, weave the thread through the protruding beads on the first and last rows to finish off securely.

MAKING THE ROUND RING

4 Continue to add beads, picking up the same color that the thread will go through next (pick up a red and take the needle through a red bead, pick up a green and take the needle through a green bead).

5 Continue to build up the pattern until the tube is about 4 inches long.

6 Finish off by taking the thread through the last three beads at the end to close the tube.

7 Thread on the 10mm bead and tie the working thread with the tail. Thread the ends back through the large bead and several rocailles before cutting them off neatly.

1 Take a long length of beading thread and pick up one red bead, one green bead, and one silver bead. Leaving a tail of about 3 inches, tie the thread to form a circle and go back through one of the beads to hide the thread.

This napkin ring was made in exactly the same way but with a background of green rocailles. This pattern looks just as effective with a background of red.

LOOMWORK BRACELET

Although it looks complicated, loomwork is a straightforward technique. You can arrange the beads in almost any pattern, but this simple geometric design is especially eye-catching.

YOU WILL NEED
•

Beads and findings
- ½ ounce blue opaque rocaille beads, size 8/0
- ½ ounce red opaque rocaille beads, size 8/0
- ½ ounce orange opaque rocaille beads, size 8/0
- ½ ounce yellow opaque rocaille beads, size 8/0
- ½ ounce black opaque rocaille beads, size 8/0
- Waxed beading thread
- Beading needle

Other equipment
- Small bead loom (see pages 58–59)
- 16 feet silk thread
- Beeswax

MAKING THE BRACELET

1 Warp nine rows of silk thread onto the beading loom, following the manufacturer's instructions. Make sure that all the threads are as tight as possible and that they are arranged neatly around the separators. Wind any excess length around one of the end pieces.

2 Figure out how much beading thread you will need by multiplying the width of the warping threads by the number of rows in the pattern. Add on about 12 inches. Run the beading thread across some beeswax to make it easier to work with.

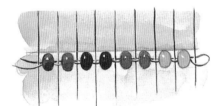

3 Thread a length of beading thread onto the needle and pick up the first line of beads – two blue, two red, two orange, two yellow – and push them to the end of the thread, leaving a tail of approximately 2 inches.

This bracelet was also made on a loom. The outermost rows taper off for a more sophisticated finish.

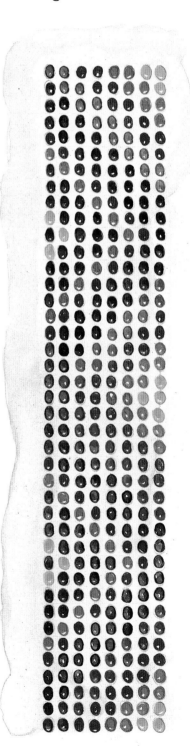

4 Bring the beads under the warping threads on the loom and push them up between each thread. Take the thread back through all the beads, making sure it is on top of the warping threads.

5 Tie the working thread to the tail end.

6 Continue to work the rows of beads, using the colors shown on the chart.

7 When you have completed the pattern, finish off all the tails by running each end back through five beads.

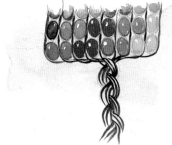

8 Cut the work off the loom, leaving the warp threads long. Separate the threads into three groups of three at each end and braid them together. Tie a knot in the end of the braids to stop them unraveling.

LOOMWORK PENDANT

Black and orange always look good together, but whatever colors you use, keep to just two strongly contrasting shades to create a dramatic effect for this fashionable pendant.

YOU WILL NEED

•

Beads and findings

- ¼ ounce orange, silver-lined rocaille beads, size 8/0
- ¾ ounce black rocaille beads, size 8/0
- ⅛ ounce opaque orange rocaille beads, size 8/0
- 11 × 8mm black beads
- Beading needle
- Waxed beading thread
- Silk thread

Other equipment

- Small bead loom (see pages 58–59)
- Scissors

MAKING THE PENDANT

1 Thread the bead loom with 22 warp threads, each approximately 39 inches long.

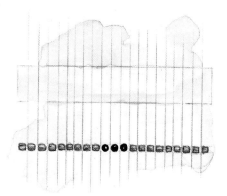

2 Starting with a long piece of beading thread, pick up nine silver-lined orange, three black, and nine silver-lined orange beads. Begin at one end of the loom with about 6 inches warping thread so that the longest ends are at the other end (and leave a tail about 3 inches long on the working thread). Take the beads under the loom. Push the beads up between the warp threads, then take the thread back through the beads, this time above the warp threads. Tie the two ends firmly together.

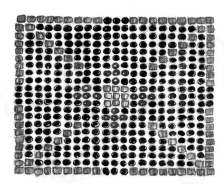

3 Continue to add rows of beads to complete the pattern as shown in the illustration.

4 When the pattern is complete, finish off the working thread and tail securely. Cut the work from the loom, leaving the warp threads long to allow for the strands and drops.

MAKING THE STRANDS

1 Working with the longest threads, finish off the middle 14 threads by running them through the outer edge of beads (using a needle). Leave four long ends at each edge.

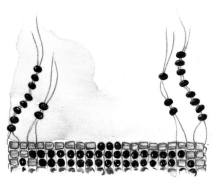

2 Join the two outside long threads together and thread through a needle, then pick up black beads until the strand measures about 12 inches. Repeat on the other side. Tie the four threads securely together and run each of the threads back through 15–20 beads to finish off. Repeat the previous step with the inner four threads.

MAKING THE DROPS

1 Working on the end of the pendant with the short threads, pick up nine black, one silver-lined orange, 10 black, and one orange rocaille. Pick up an 8mm black bead and one orange rocaille. Miss the last rocaille and take the thread back through the black bead and the 21 rocailles, finishing it off by tying it to the next thread. Finish off both ends by running each through several beads.

2 Make 10 more drops, spacing them evenly along the bottom edge of the pendant.

LOOMWORK BELT

The materials and design shown here will make a decorative beaded panel about 21½ inches long. If you want to make it longer, add extra rows of plain rocailles at both ends.

MAKING THE BELT

1 Thread your loom with 16 lengths of warping thread, each approximately 3 feet long.

2 Thread a long length of beading thread on a needle and pick up 15 turquoise rocailles. Leaving a tail of approximately 3 inches, take the beads under the warp threads, then making sure you go over the warp threads, pick up each bead in turn. Fasten the working thread securely to the tail.

3 Repeat step 2 to add a second row of 15 turquoise rocailles.

4 Begin to follow the pattern for the bird motif, making sure that you have 15 rocailles in each row.

5 When you have completed the bird, work two rows of turquoise rocailles, then follow the chart for the small diamond, add one row of turquoise and follow the chart for the large diamond. Add one row of turquoise, then repeat the small diamond.

6 Work two rows of turquoise rocailles, then work another bird motif.

7 Work two rows of turquoise rocailles before the next group of diamond motifs, then work two more rows of turquoise rocailles.

8 Work the third bird motif, this time turning its head to face in the other direction. Complete the bird and work two rows of turquoise rocailles.

9 Remove the work from the loom and take each thread back through five or six beads before cutting it off. Do not take a thread back through a complete row of beads or the threads will be too bulky.

10 Glue the finished beaded panel to a leather belt.

You need only a fairly short loom because the threads are wrapped at the sides and can be moved along as necessary.

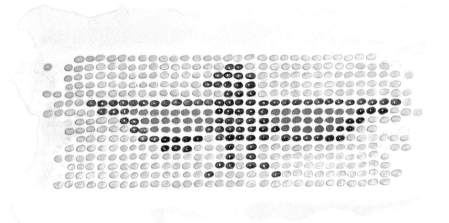

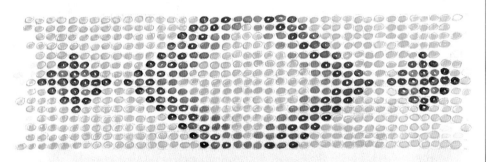

YOU WILL NEED
•

Beads and findings
- 3 ounces turquoise opaque rocaille beads, size 8/0
- ¾ ounce black opaque rocaille beads, size 8/0
- ¾ ounce orange opaque rocaille beads, size 8/0
- ¼ ounce red opaque rocaille beads, size 8/0
- ¼ ounce blue opaque rocaille beads, size 8/0
- Silk thread
- Waxed beading thread
- Beading needle

Other equipment
- Small bead loom (see pages 58–59)
- Scissors
- Plain leather belt, approximately 1½ inches wide
- Clear, all-purpose glue

GUNMETAL CHOKER

This loomwork panel measures 9 inches and the bead loop fastening extends the length to fit a neck that measures between 11½–13½ inches.

YOU WILL NEED
•

Beads and findings
- ½ ounce gunmetal rocaille beads, size 12/0
- ¾ ounce gunmetal bugles
- 4 × 8mm facet beads
- 1 × 6mm facet bead
- Silk thread
- Waxed beading thread
- Beading needle

Other equipment
- Small bead loom (see pages 58–59)
- Scissors

MAKING THE CHOKER

1 Thread 12 warp threads, each approximately 39 inches long, onto the loom, positioning them so that the first two are close together with a gap long enough to accommodate a bugle before the next two, which should be close together for a rocaille. You should have enough gaps to allow for five rows of bugles.

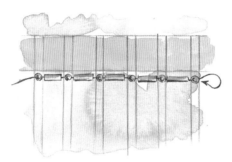

2 Leaving a tail of approximately 3 inches, pick up alternately one rocaille and one bugle until you have five bugles on the thread. Pick up one rocaille. Take the thread under the loom and push the beads up between the warp threads.

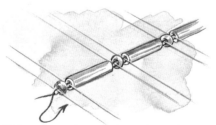

3 Taking the working thread over the warp threads, go back through all 11 beads. Tie the working thread to the end.

4 Repeat for a total of 29 rows of alternate rocailles and bugles for the first section.

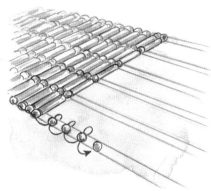

5 Pick up one rocaille, go under the first two warp threads and back through the rocaille. Repeat this 10 more times along the top row, for a total of 11 rocailles.

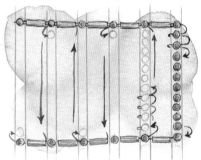

6 Complete a vertical row of alternating rocailles and bugles, as in step 2. For the second linking row of rocailles, carry the working thread down through the first rocaille, bugle, and next rocaille so that you can fill the next horizontal row with 11 rocailles.

7 Work the other four horizontal linking rows, then complete the central section of vertical bugles and rocailles, working 29 rows in total, as in steps 2–3.

8 Repeat steps 5–7 once more. Finish off the tail of your working thread and cut from the loom.

9 Leave the four central warp threads at each end. Finish off all the other threads, taking each through several beads before cutting.

10 Using two threads at one end for the clasp, pick up 18 rocailles, one 8mm bead, six rocailles, one 8mm bead, six rocailles, one 8mm bead, six rocailles, one 8mm bead, and one rocaille. Miss the last rocaille and take both threads back through all, including the first 8mm bead. Pick up 18 rocailles and tie the threads to the other two remaining threads. Finish off by threading the ends through several beads before cutting.

11 At the other end, pick up 18 rocailles on two threads. Pick up one 6mm bead, then approximately 21 rocailles to make a loop. Check that it will fit over the 8mm beads at the other end before taking the thread back through the 6mm bead. Pick up 18 rocailles and tie the two threads to the two remaining threads. Finish off securely.

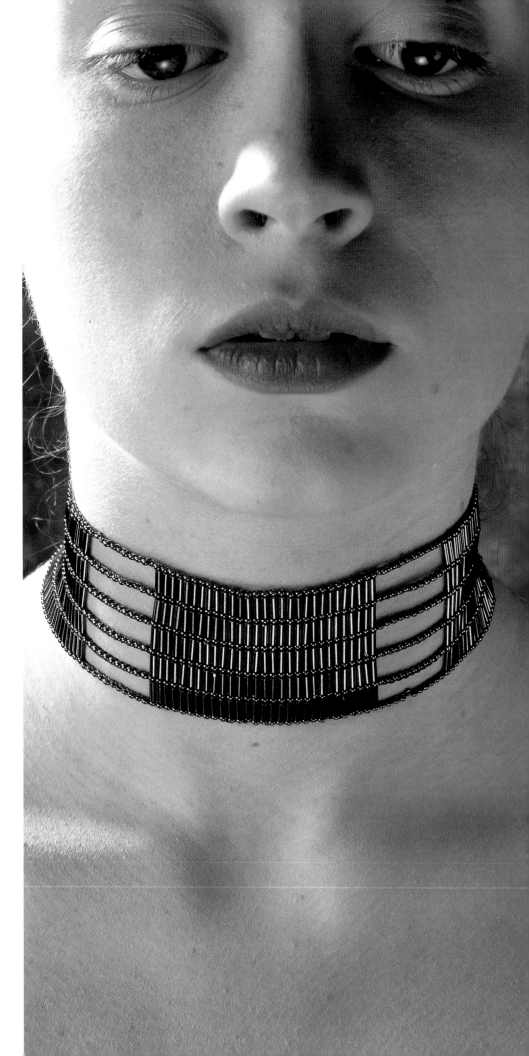

BEAD

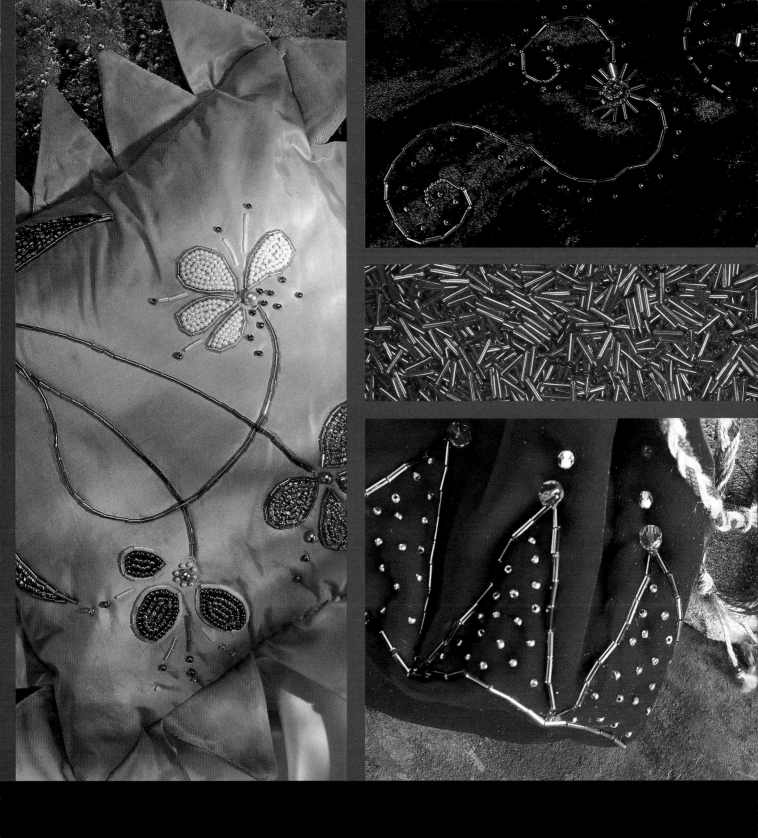

EMBROIDERY

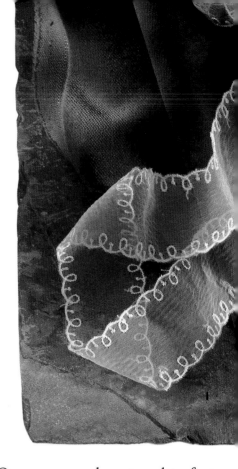

Beads have been sewn onto clothing for many centuries. Embroidery with tiny glass beads is synonymous with native American and African clothing and artifacts and with the elegant dresses and accessories of the 19th century. Bead embroidery can be a simple process or a highly skilled art, and the projects that follow will help you to develop your own skills.

EQUIPMENT Before you start any bead embroidery you need to work out your design. You can either draw straight onto your garment or fabric using tailor's pencil or with a water-erasable marking pen. Or you can make a template first. Simply work out your design on a grid and transfer the design to tracing paper. Next, go over the outline on the back of the tracing paper with tailor's pencil, place the piece of tracing paper onto your fabric and rub down the design from the front of the tracing paper, leaving the pencil ready for the embroidery. You can also use beads to emphasize the patterns on fabric or lace, as in our camisole project (page 98). Use silk thread or unwaxed polyester thread for embroidery, with a needle that suits your choice of beads. These should be fine, without being too weak.

Fig. 1

TECHNIQUES There are two basic methods for bead embroidery. Individual beads can be sewn to the fabric – in much the same way as a button would be attached – using a back - stitch (*fig. 1*). When covering large areas, two beads (instead of one) can be attached. This is useful for making straight lines. Couching is another method; string the beads onto a length of thread, lay this onto the design, then secure the thread between the beads with another thread that is worked from the back of the fabric (*fig. 2*). This method is very good for large designs. A variation involves working from one side of the pattern to the other with exactly the right number of beads strung onto a thread, but this is not suitable for very large designs.

Fig. 2

TYPES OF BEADS Most bead embroidery is done with rocailles and bugles, but any light beads can be used — in the past, embroidery was also done with tiny ostrich shell disks or with pearls. You must think about the suitability of your beads before you begin. Beads used for embroidery should be colorfast if they are destined for garments. The only truly colorfast beads are those that have the color in the glass. Some beads, such as colored wood, will even run in the rain, and colors can be affected by perspiration. Most coated rocailles or imitation pearls will eventually lose some of their original qualities with washing or cleaning. No beaded garment should ever be washed in hot water as the beading thread may shrink and tighten the design. Don't be put off though — given gentle hand-washing, garments embroidered with colorfast beads should last for years.

Once you have started you will probably get "hooked" on the possibilities of bead embroidery. You can embroider most fabrics unless they are very fine or very stiff. You can also use knitted garments – sometimes it is better to back the inside of the beaded areas with fabric. Always work in a good light and have your equipment to hand. Bead embroidery can add splendor to a special piece of clothing or an ordinary accessory, and it could also be a unique way to cope with a small stain or burn on a favorite garment.

1 Lace and fabric for embroidery
2 Bead-embroidered ribbon
3 Beading thread
4 Water-erasable markers
5 Bugles
6 Rocailles
7 Sequins
8 Tracing paper

BEADED HAT

*Use braid and beads on this pillbox hat to match your clothes
and make yourself the center of attention. The same method
could be used to decorate a beret.*

YOU WILL NEED
•
Beads and thread
- 6 flat, triangular, red beads
- ⅛ ounce, red, two-cut, silver-lined rocaille beads, size 12/0
- 1 large round flat red bead
- Beading thread
Other equipment
- 1 plain pillbox hat
- Water-erasable marking pen
- Ruler
- Approximately 8 feet black braid
- Dressmaker's pins
- Sewing needle

ATTACHING THE TRIM

1 Find the central point on the top of the hat and use the pen to mark it. Draw two equilateral triangles, with sides about 2½ inches long, so that the corners form a six-pointed star and the center of the star is at the center of the hat. Extend the corners of the triangles to form loops.

2 Starting at one corner, pin the braid along the lines of one of the triangles and around the loops. Sew the braid in place. Repeat with the other triangle and loops.

3 Use the marking pen to make a regular zigzag pattern around the edge of the hat. On our hat, each line was about 1½ inches long. Pin, then stitch the braid in place.

ADDING THE BEADS

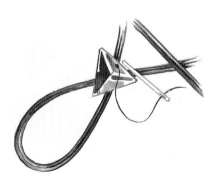

1 Sew a red triangular bead to each of the points of the star.

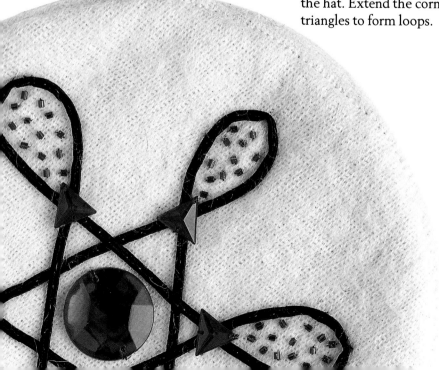

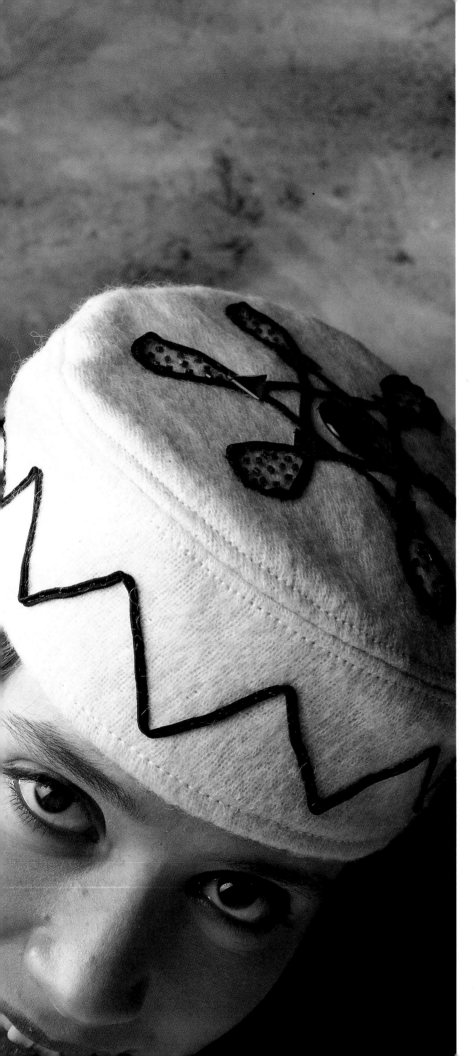

2 Sew individual rocailles in a random pattern in the middle of each of the loops, taking the thread through to the inside of the hat after attaching each bead.

3 Sew the large round bead in the middle of the star.

Beads and braid in contrasting colors were used here, but you could also try matching the colors, for example all black, which would make it easier to pair the hat with any outfit.

CAMISOLE

*Choose a camisole that has three or four large flower motifs
rather than several small ones, which will be difficult to work
with and will look less effective.*

YOU WILL NEED

•

Beads and thread

- Approximately 500 × 2.5mm pearls
- ⅛ ounce 5mm sequins
- 8 small crystal drops with top holes
- ⅛ ounce transparent rocaille beads, size 12/0 (optional)
- Unwaxed beading thread

Other equipment

- Camisole with lace top
- Scissors
- Beading needle

ADDING THE BEADS

1 Take a length of thread, not too long, tie a knot in the end and make a small stitch on the wrong side of the camisole. Take the thread through to the front.

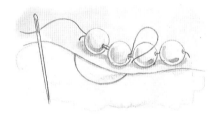

2 Pick up four pearl beads and lay them flat against the material, curving them slightly to form part of a circle. Take the needle through to the back, bring it through to the front between the second and third beads. Take the thread through the last two beads and pick up two more beads. Continue to work in this way to complete the circle.

3 Using the same method as in step 2, outline one side of the leaf or petal shapes with pearl beads, curving the line gently. Do not add too many beads or their weight will pull the garment out of shape.

4 With a new length of thread, attach sequins to the other petals. Bring the thread through to the right side, pick up a sequin, cup-shaped side facing upward, then take the thread through to the wrong side near to the edge of the sequin. Bring the thread through to the right side close to your previous stitch and pick up a second sequin, which will overlap the first sequin.

5 Continue to add lines of sequins in this way.

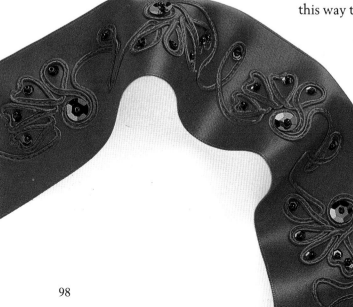

Sequins and rocailles in a darker shade add a dramatic touch.

6 Finally, sew two crystal drops to the middle of the pearl circles. Take your thread through each bead twice to make sure that it is held firmly.

7 Some of the sequins can be attached with rocailles. Bring your thread through to the right side, pick up a sequin, cup-shaped side up, pick up a rocaille and take your thread back through the sequin so that the rocaille holds the sequin in place. If you use this method, the edges of the sequins should just touch, not overlap.

PEARL-STUDDED PINCUSHION

Decorate a simple pincushion with delicate beads to transform a functional object into a pretty ornament.

YOU WILL NEED

•

Beads and thread
- ½ ounce pale blue bugles
- ½ ounce silver bugles
- ½ ounce lilac-colored bugles
- 5 × 5mm sea-green pearl beads
- 12 × 3mm dark green pearl beads
- 4 × 10mm glass drop beads
- ½ ounce 2mm pearl beads
- Beading thread to match pincushion

Other equipment
- Pincushion, approximately 4 × 4 inches
- Scissors
- Beading needle

DECORATING THE PINCUSHION

1 Tie a knot in the end of a long length of beading thread and take it into one corner of the pincushion. Thread on a sufficient number of pale blue bugles to reach along one edge and take your needle in and out of the next corner.

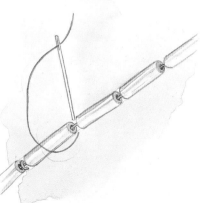

2 Keep this row of bugles in place by making tiny stitches between each bugle to hold down the working thread. Finish off the thread with several tiny stitches in the corner.

3 Repeat steps 1 and 2 to decorate the other three sides.

4 Attach diagonal rows of alternating silver and lilac bugles across the top of the pincushion in the same way.

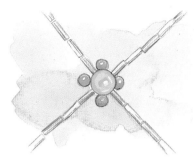

5 Using a new length of thread, attach one large sea-green bead at the center of the front and four 3mm dark green beads around the large bead.

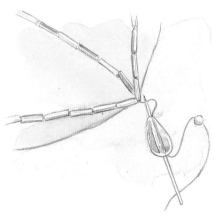

6 Attach a length of knotted thread to a corner of the pincushion and pick up a drop bead and a 2mm pearl bead. Take the thread back through the drop bead and make one or two small stitches in the corner. Stitch on a sea-green bead and a 3mm dark green bead on either side above the drop bead. Repeat on the other three corners.

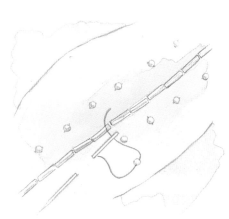

7 Stitch a row of 2mm pearl beads all around the edge of the pincushion, positioning them about ⅛ inch from the bugles along the edge and about ¼ inch apart.

8 Decorate the back of the pincushion by stitching 2mm pearl beads over the back, spacing them evenly but in a random pattern.

Another pincushion has been decorated with pearlized rocailles, pink bugles, and five large lilac-colored pearl beads. There are clear glass drop beads at the corners.

EMBROIDERED CARD

Although this little card seems to need a lot of beads and sequins, it is quite easy to make and it would be the ideal way of using up any leftover sequins and rocailles.

SEWING ON THE BEADS

1 Fold the piece of fabric in four to find the middle, creasing it lightly at this point. This is the middle of the fourth row of green rocailles. Count back three squares.

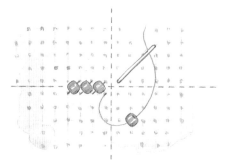

2 Bring your needle through to the right side in the bottom left-hand corner of the square, pick up a green rocaille and take the needle through the top right-hand corner of the square. Add six more individually stitched rocailles in the same way.

3 Work downward to add three more rows of rocailles, increasing the number by two in each row, so that there are 13 green rocailles in the bottom row.

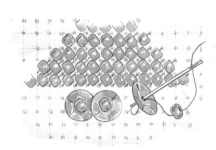

4 Miss one row of fabric and find the central square on the next row. Bring the needle to the front through the middle of the square and pick up a green sequin and a green rocaille. Take the needle back through the sequin and the fabric.

5 Miss one square to the right of the first sequin and add a second green sequin and rocaille in the same way. Repeat to the left of the central sequin.

6 Working downward, missing a square of fabric between each sequin and adding two sequins in each row, work three more rows of sequins and rocailles. There will be nine sequins and rocailles in the final row.

7 Bring the needle through the bottom right-hand corner of the central square in the final row of sequins. Pick up a bronze bugle and stitch it vertically in place. Bring the needle through the bottom left-hand corner of the central square and attach a second vertical bronze bugle in the same way.

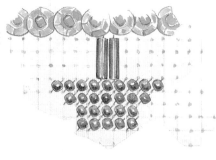

8 In the row immediately under the bugles, stitch nine bronze rocailles. Under this, stitch a row of seven rocailles and two rows of five rocailles. Fasten off the thread.

YOU WILL NEED
•

Beads and thread
- ⅛ ounce green silver-lined rocaille beads, size 12/0
- ⅛ ounce 4mm green sequins
- 2 × 6mm bronze bugles
- ⅛ ounce bronze rocaille beads, size 12/0
- ⅛ ounce red silver-lined rocaille beads, size 12/0
- 7 × 6mm gold bugles
- 21 orange silver-lined rocaille beads, size 12/0
- Beading thread

Other equipment
- Piece of white embroidery fabric, approximately 4 × 3 inches
- Scissors
- Beading needle
- Clear, all-purpose glue
- Ready-made blank card
- Clothespins or masking tape

We have used green two-cut rocailles and red and yellow size 12/0 rocailles to make this pretty bookmark, although the same pattern would look delightful around the collar of a plain blouse.

9 Return to the middle of the tree and finish off the triangle of rocailles with a row of five rocailles and a row of three rocailles above it.

10 Work the top section of the tree with three rows of sequins and rocailles, this time working one row of five, one row of three, and a single sequin and rocaille at the top.

11 Add some randomly placed red rocailles among the sequins at the top and bottom of the tree. We have added five in the bottom section and two at the top.

12 Bring the thread through to the front just above one of the outside sequins and pick up a gold bugle. Stitch the bugle down and add a red rocaille at its top and three orange rocaille around as a "flame." Repeat this on the other points of the tree.

13 Check that the tree motif will be visible in the opening of the card, trimming the fabric if necessary. Glue the edges of the fabric to the ready-made card so that the motif is centrally positioned in the front. Hold with clothespins or masking tape until the glue is dry.

DECORATED CUSHION

You can copy the design shown here or create your own to decorate a cushion. We used smooth fabric because a textured or patterned background would divert attention from the beads.

DECORATING THE CUSHION

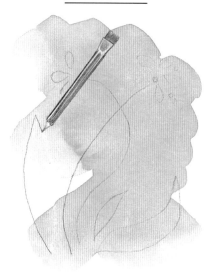

1 Draw the pattern on the fabric with the tailor's chalk pencil. If you are using a piece of fabric that will later be made into a cushion, mount the material in a slate frame of the kind designed to hold canvas for needlepoint. If you are using a ready-made cushion cover, try to keep the fabric smooth and taut with an embroidery ring, which you can move around as you complete each section.

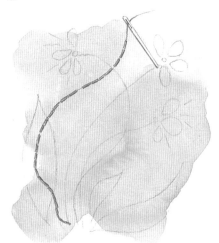

2 Using a long length of thread, bring your needle through to the front and pick up enough grass green bugles to make the first stem. Lay the beads along your drawn line and take the thread through to the wrong side.

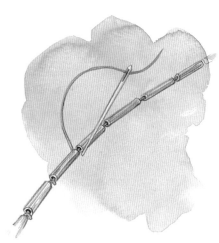

3 Bring the needle back through to the right side and make a tiny stitch between each bugle to hold down the thread. Finish off the thread with tiny overstitches on the wrong side.

4 Complete the other stems and the outlines of the leaves in the same way, finishing off the thread with tiny overstitches on the wrong side of the fabric.

YOU WILL NEED
•
Beads and thread
- ½ ounce grass green bugles
- ½ ounce light green rocaille beads, size 8/0
- ½ ounce dark green rocaille beads, size 8/0
- ½ ounce opaque green rocaille beads, size 12/0
- ½ ounce opalescent bugles
- ½ ounce metallic lilac bugles
- ½ ounce pink bugles
- ½ ounce 2mm pearl beads
- ½ ounce bronze rocaille beads, size 8/0
- ½ ounce metallic pink rocaille beads, size 8/0
- ½ ounce metallic green rocaille beads, size 8/0
- ½ ounce metallic green rocaille beads, size 12/0
- Approximately 30 × 5mm assorted pearl beads
- Beading thread to match cushion
  Other equipment
- Cushion cover, approximately 12 × 12 inches
- Tailor's pencil
- Scissors
- Beading needle

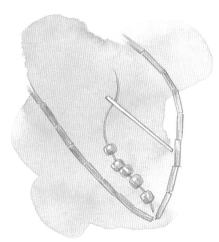

5 Use different kinds of green rocailles to fill in the leaves. Take a length of knotted thread through to the right side and pick up about five beads. Take the thread back to the wrong side, make a small stitch and take the needle back to the front. Repeat with another five beads, continuing until you have completely filled the area.

6 Outline the shapes of the petals in the same way as you outlined the leaves, but this time using opalescent, lilac, and pink bugles.

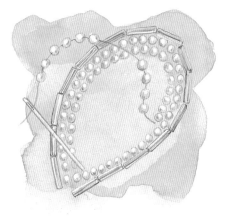

7 Fill in the shapes of the petals in the same way as you filled in the leaves, but this time use the 2mm pearl beads and the bronze, metallic pink, and metallic green rocailles.

8 Taking a long length of thread, add pearl beads and bugles around the flowers to create the stamens and centers of the flowers.

9 Our cushion has a fringe of points around the edge, and we added a bead to each point.

VELVET EVENING BAG

Stitching beads on a plain evening bag is an easy way of adding sparkle and glamour. Small beads at the end of the drawstring make for a festive touch.

DECORATING THE BAG

1 Use a tape measure and pins or tailor's pencil to mark a row of triangles around the base of the bag.
2 Take a length of thread and tie a knot in the end. Take the thread through from the inside of the bag to the bottom of one of the triangles around the base.

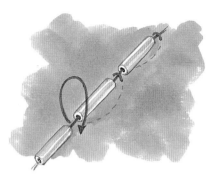

4 Taking the needle through to the inside of the bag each time, secure the row of bugles in place by making a tiny stitch between each bead to hold the thread down. Finish off the thread neatly and securely at the end of the row, on the inside of the bag.
5 Repeat steps 2–4 to complete the sides of all the triangles.
6 Using green bugles and the same technique, add the row of beads all around the base of the bag.

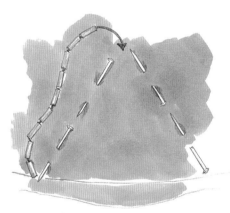

3 Pick up approximately eight green bugles. Take the needle through the apex of the triangle and pull the thread until the beads are lying flat against the fabric.

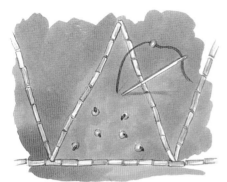

7 Using a new length of thread with a knot in the end, bring your needle through from the inside of the bag and begin to add the green rocailles in a random pattern inside each of the triangles. Stitch each rocaille in position individually and use about 20 in each triangle. Finish off the thread securely after completing each triangle.

8 Use a new length of thread to attach an amber and a clear bead and a red rocaille to the apex of each triangle. Finish off the thread securely each time.

9 Stitch green rocaille beads around the top of the bag, placing them about ¼ inch apart.

10 Using individual lengths of thread, attach a large green bead and a red rocaille to the tip of the triangular points around the top of the bag. Take the thread up through the green bead and the rocaille, then down through the green bead only.

11 If your bag has a drawstring, add some matching faceted beads and rocailles to the ends of the tassels and secure with knots.

DAISY VEST

We have used bronze-colored rocailles and bugle beads to adorn this plain black velvet vest, and you could repeat the pattern around the hem of a matching skirt.

MAKING THE DAISIES

1 Use the pencil to draw a design on the vest. Mark the centers of the daisies, then draw a circle approximately 1¼ inches in diameter from the center of each.

2 Begin a daisy by securing the thread to the wrong side of the fabric and bringing it through to the front at the center of a daisy.

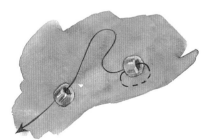

3 Pick up one 8/0 brown rocaille, take the thread back through the fabric so that the bead lies flat. Bring the thread back through to the right side at the same point and go back through the bead.

4 Repeat step 3 twice more to form a triangle of rocailles.

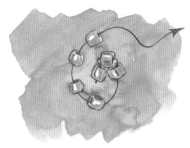

5 Pick up four 8/0 brown rocailles and coil these around the triangle. Push the beads tightly together, holding them in place by bringing the thread back through the third and fourth rocailles.

6 Repeat step 5 until the daisy center is as large as you wish. We used 22–24 rocailles.

7 Form the petals by bringing the thread through to the front at the edge of the circle. Sew on a bugle. We used 15–17 bugles on each daisy.

8 Repeat steps 1–7 to complete the other daisies.

3 Form the swirls at each end by picking up about four 12/0 rocailles at a time. Sew them on the fabric and go back through the last two. We used 10–13 rocailles in all.

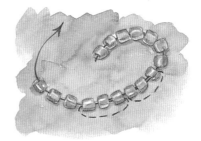

4 Make the bottom swirl from 12/0 rocailles. Pick up four rocailles at a time, and go back through the last two or three until you have completed the design.

5 Finish each swirl with an outline of dots by sewing single 8/0 bronze rocailles at evenly spaced intervals. Secure the thread at the back and sew on each rocaille individually.

MAKING THE SWIRLS

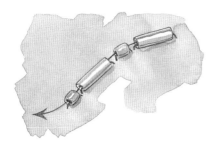

1 Make the top swirl by securing the thread at the back and bringing it through to the front at the top of the daisy. Sew on one bugle, going through it twice, leave a 1/8 inch gap and sew on a 8/0 brown rocaille. Complete the pattern, alternating bugles and 8/0 rocailles. Finish with 13 8/0 rocailles as before.

2 Make the middle swirl by threading on one 12/0 rocaille, one bugle, and one 12/0 rocaille. Lay them flat along the design and take the needle to the back of the material. Come back up and take the thread through the bugle and last rocaille. Continue to work the design by picking up a bugle and a 12/0 rocaille, sewing as before.

SHOE PATCHES

The quantities given here are sufficient to make one pair of beaded shoe patches. Use half the quantity and the same technique to make a decoration for a handbag or a garment.

YOU WILL NEED
•
Beads and thread
- 2 turquoise sequins
- ½ ounce silver rocaille beads, size 12/0
- ½ ounce turquoise rocaille beads, size 12/0
- 120 turquoise bugles
- 60 silver bugles
- Beading thread

Other equipment
- 1 pair of shoe clips
- Medium-weight iron-on black interfacing, 4 pieces each 4 × 4 inches
- Medium-weight black fabric, 2 pieces each 4 × 4 inches
- Pattern paper
- Scissors
- Beading needle
- Tailor's pencil
- Clear, all-purpose glue (optional)

MAKING THE PATCHES

1 Iron a piece of interfacing to the wrong side of one square of fabric. Draw a circle with a diameter of about 2 inches on a piece of pattern paper and cut it out. Place this on the fabric and draw around the outline with a tailor's pencil. Do not cut out the circle yet.

2 Find the center of the circle and bring the thread through to the front. Pick up a turquoise sequin and a silver bead. Take the thread back through the sequin so that the bead holds it in place.

3 Bring the needle through to the front, close to the edge of the sequin, and pick up two turquoise rocailles. Lay them flat on the fabric, curving them around the sequin, and take the needle to the wrong side of the fabric. Bring it back through to the front between the rocailles and take the thread through the second rocaille. Pick up two more rocailles and continue in this way until you have completed the circle.

Patches can also be made from shapes, with metallic thread and braid to complement the shimmery beads.

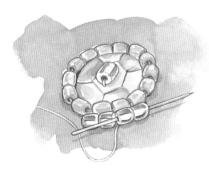

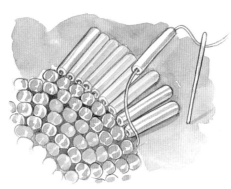

4 Make a circle of 12/0 silver rocailles next. Bring the needle through to the front of the fabric and pick up four beads. Lay these against the turquoise rocailles and take the needle through to the back. Bring it to the front between the second and third silver beads and take the thread through the third and fourth beads before picking up four more beads. Continue in this way until you have completed the circle.

5 Continue to work circles of alternating turquoise and silver rocailles until you have four complete circles of each.

6 In the next circle, pick up four silver rocailles, securing them as before, then four turquoise rocailles. Repeat the groups of four, alternating the colors around the circle.

7 On the next row, alternate groups of four silver rocailles with five turquoise rocailles.

8 Work two complete circles with silver. The final row of silver should be approximately on the chalk circle.

9 Bring your needle through to the right side as close to the circle of silver beads as possible and pick up a turquoise bugle. This should be positioned at 90 degrees to the silver bead, and the base of the bugle should touch the silver bead. Take your needle through to the wrong side to hold the bugle in position and bring it back through to the right side, as close as possible to the next silver bead. Pick up another turquoise bugle and stitch it in place so that there is a tiny gap between the bugles at the ouside edge. Continue to add bugles all around the circle. We used alternating groups of six turquoise and three silver bugles.

10 Cover up the stitches on the back of the finished pieces by carefully ironing on a second piece of interfacing.

11 Using very sharp scissors, trim away the excess fabric and interfacing to within 1/8 inch of the bugles.

12 Stitch or glue a shoe clip to the back of each circle.

GLUING AND

PINNING

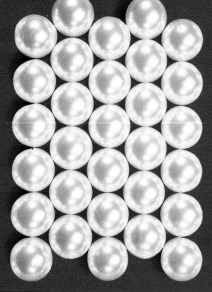

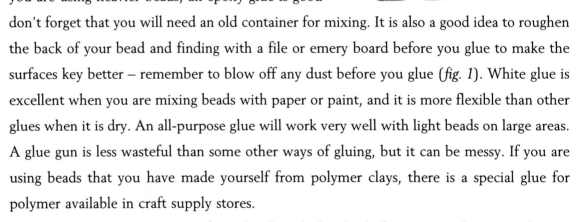

Beads are usually associated with jewelry making and embroidery, but you mustn't forget that with a little creativity, their uses can extend beyond stringing and sewing. The projects in this chapter will help inspire you to use beads in other ways. When you use your imagination and become a compulsive beader, you too will be inspired to think of many other decorative uses for the enormous variety of attractive beads that are available.

EQUIPMENT It is important to choose the right glue. If you are using heavier beads, an epoxy glue is good – don't forget that you will need an old container for mixing. It is also a good idea to roughen the back of your bead and finding with a file or emery board before you glue to make the surfaces key better – remember to blow off any dust before you glue (*fig. 1*). White glue is excellent when you are mixing beads with paper or paint, and it is more flexible than other glues when it is dry. An all-purpose glue will work very well with light beads on large areas. A glue gun is less wasteful than some other ways of gluing, but it can be messy. If you are using beads that you have made yourself from polymer clays, there is a special glue for polymer available in craft supply stores.

Test one or two of your beads with the glue before you use them to make sure that the glue will not remove the finish or the coating from the beads. As with all the projects in this book, you should work in a good light — an adjustable desk lamp on your work

Fig. 1

Fig. 2

surface is ideal. Work in a well-ventilated room when using glue. Collect all your materials and equipment together before you start and, especially with gluing, find a place where your work-in-progress can be left undisturbed.

Gluing and pinning are ideal for decorative projects that will not have a large amount of wear, you do not want to glue anything that will have to be washed or cleaned. Don't forget that you can use gluing in simple ways too – gluing a cabochon onto a flat-back finding will make a lovely brooch in no time at all. You can make original hatpins and stickpins by putting a little glue onto a long stiffened pin and then threading on beads. You can buy special hatpins and stickpins with a safety end cover from bead shops. It is a good idea to put a French crimp bead on after the beads as well as the glue (*fig. 2*).

1 *Contact adhesive*
2 *Epoxy resin*
3 *All-purpose glue*
4 *File*
5 *Dressmaker's pins*
6 *Hatpins with*
  safety end covers

Harlequin Mask

Masks used to be worn at balls so that strangers could flirt, untrammeled by conventions. Use a mix of beads and sequins to revive an old custom and transform a plain mask.

YOU WILL NEED
•
Beads
- I packet green sequins
- I packet turquoise sequins
- I packet blue sequins
- I packet purple sequins
- I packet pink sequins
- I packet light pink sequins
- I packet silver bugle beads
- I packet gold bugle beads
- I packet red bugle beads
- I packet blue bugle beads
- I packet transparent rocaille beads
- I packet gold rocaille beads
- I packet metallic purple rocaille beads
- I packet small gold beads
- 8 flat, mirrored beads (we used four triangles, two squares, and two ovals)
- Beading thread
- Beading needle

Other equipment
- Tailor's pencil
- I mask
- Clear, all-purpose glue
- I silver glitter glue pen
- I gold glitter glue pen

DECORATING THE MASK

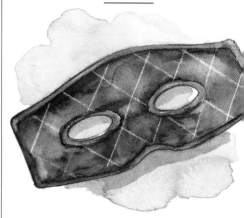

1 Use the tailor's pencil to draw a harlequin-style diamond grid onto the mask, leaving ¼ inch border all around the edge and around the eye holes.

2 Work on one diamond-shape at a time. Apply a thin layer of glue to the mask, then carefully apply sequins, one by one, using a needle. Overlap them slightly until you have covered the whole diamond.

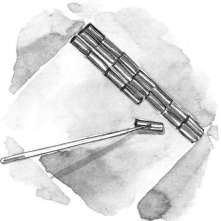

3 When you apply the bugle beads, use a beading needle to guide them into position. Add one bead at a time and finish one row at a time.

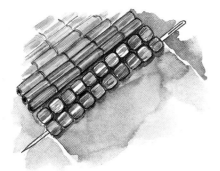

4 Thread sufficient rocailles on a needle to cover one edge of a diamond-shape. Continue until you have covered the whole diamond.
5 Achieve a variety of effects by gluing down the beads in different directions within individual diamonds.
6 Fill in some of the diamonds with glitter glue pens, using as many techniques and colors as you wish to create an interesting, multi-colored surface.

MAKING THE DROPS

1 Make the beaded drops by gluing two flat, mirrored beads together, making sure that the holes in the beads match up. Leave to dry.

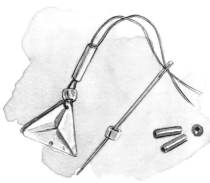

2 Cut approximately 31 inches of beading thread and thread it through the glued mirror beads until they are about halfway along. Bring the two ends together and thread both strands through the eye of a beading needle. Thread a variety of rocailles and bugle beads onto the double strand until they reach the desired length. Sew the thread on the back of the mask.
3 Repeat step 2 three more times to make a total of four strands. These do not have to be equal in length.

PICTURE FRAME

You can paint a plain wooden frame with silver before you begin. Spray paint or modelmaker's silver paint work well, but leave the paint to dry before you start to glue.

YOU WILL NEED

•

Beads
- 3 flat round 30mm silver beads
- 1 flat round 25mm blue bead
- 1 flat round 25mm amethyst bead
- 2 flat round 12mm amethyst beads
- 5 flat round 12mm silver beads
- 19 flat square silver beads
- 3 flat square blue beads
- 5 flat square amethyst beads
- 12 flat triangular silver beads
- 2 flat diamond-shaped turquoise beads
- 8 flat oval blue beads
- 1 ounce 8mm silver bugle beads
- 1 ounce 12mm silver bugle beads
- 1 ounce 5mm blue bugle beads
- 1 packet transparent rocaille beads
- 1 packet blue rocaille beads
- 1 packet turquoise rocaille beads

Other equipment
- 1 picture frame, 9½ × 8 inches, with sides ½ inch wide
- 1 sheet plain, white paper, slightly larger than frame
- Beading needle
- Pencil
- Clear, all-purpose glue

DECORATING THE FRAME

1 Place the frame on the sheet of paper and use a pencil to trace the outlines of the inner and outer edges.

2 Using the outline as a template, experiment with the arrangement of the largest flat beads first. Position the smaller first beads among the larger beads and move them around until you are satisfied with the design.

3 Lay the frame next to the template and, keeping to the pattern you have chosen, begin to glue the large beads in place. Once all the flat beads are in position, leave to dry for at least an hour.

4 Add the bugle beads one by one, working on small sections of the frame at a time. Apply a smear of glue to the frame and use a beading needle to help position the beads, which should be placed in various directions to create interesting textural effects.

5 Add the rocailles two or three at a time, with the help of a beading needle, until all the gaps have been filled. Leave to dry overnight.

When cleaning the glass, wipe the edges gently, being careful not to get any harsh detergents on the beaded frame.

CHRISTMAS BALLS

Most craft suppliers and the notions departments of large stores stock polystyrene balls. Be sure to use a thimble to protect your pinning finger when making these decorations.

ATTACHING THE RIBBON

1 Cut a piece of ribbon about 8 inches long. Pick up a silver rocaille and small purple sequin on a pin and stick the pin through the center of the ribbon.

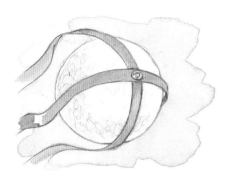

YOU WILL NEED
•
Beads
- ¼ ounce silver rocaille beads, size 12/0
- ⅛ ounce 5mm purple sequins
- ⅛ ounce 8mm purple sequins
- ⅛ ounce 5mm silver sequins
Other equipment
- 3 feet purple ribbon, ⅜ inch wide
- Clear nail polish
- Scissors
- Short dressmaker's pins
- Ruler or tape measure
- Styrofoam ball, 2½ inches in diameter
- Thimble

2 Take the remaining ribbon and measure 8 inches from one end. Pass the pin used in step 1 through this point so that the two lengths of ribbon are at right angles to each other. Stick the pin into the ball and bring the ribbons around the sides so that the surface of the ball is divided into four equal sections.

3 Bring the two short ends together at the opposite side of the ball and hold with a pin. Assemble the other ends at the same point and pin, leaving the long end loose.

Follow the same method for the purple tree decoration to make a plain pink or a plain turquoise ball. We used size 12/0 silver rocailles in each case, using smaller sequins to hold the ribbon in place.

We used an ordinary metal cookie cutter to make the basic outline for these heart-shaped decorations. Press the cutter gently into the styrofoam, then use a craft knife to cut out the shape. Kitchen equipment stores offer all sorts of shapes – stars, Christmas trees, and angels could all be made in the same way.

4 Dab nail polish on the cut end of the ribbon to prevent fraying. When dry, make a loop with the long end. Pick up a rocaille and small sequin on a pin. Use the pin to hold the three short ends and the end of the loop in place.

2 Surround the purple sequin with eight rocailles and silver sequins, and pin two small purple sequins and rocailles at the top of the circle of silver sequins. Repeat on the bottom of the circle.

DECORATING THE BALL

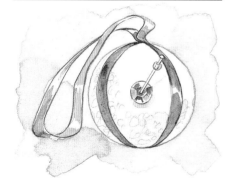

3 Pin a row of silver sequins and rocailles next to the ribbon and all around the edge of the segment.
4 Fill the remaining space with large purple sequins, keeping the rows as straight as you can.
5 Repeat until the other three sections are filled.

1 Pick up a rocaille and a large purple sequin on a pin and place them in the middle of one of the segments.

BLACKBERRY NECKLACE

This witty and delectable feast of a necklace is as much fun to make as it is to wear. When you've made this one, try a raspberry necklace!

YOU WILL NEED
•

Beads and findings
- 1 ounce purple rocaille beads, size 12/0
- 1 ounce red rocaille beads, size 12/0
- 1 ounce black rocaille beads, size 12/0
- 1 necklace hook
- 2 jump rings

Other equipment
- Fine gauge wire
- Approximately 20 styrofoam balls, ¾ inch in diameter
- Green tissue paper
- Green textured paper
- Scissors
- Clear, all-purpose glue
- Black acrylic or watercolor paint
- Paintbrush
- Epoxy glue
- Wire cutters
- Awl or bradawl

MAKING THE BERRIES

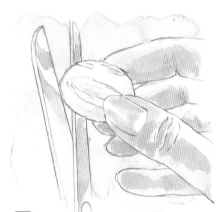

1 Trim the styrofoam balls so that they are more oblong in shape.
2 Cut some pieces of wire, about 2½ inches long, and use the all-purpose glue to stick them into the base of each oblong shape to form a stem. Paint each one black.

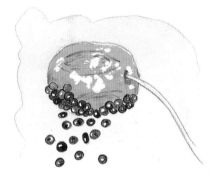

3 When the paint is dry, cover each shape with beads, sticking them on a few at a time with epoxy glue. Vary the colors so that some of the berries look "riper" than others.

MAKING THE LEAVES

1 Cut 33 leaves from tissue paper and 33 leaves from the textured paper; each leaf should be about 1½ × 1 inch. Cut 20 sepals from the textured paper; each of these should measure about 1 inch in diameter.
2 Cut 22 pieces of wire 2 inches long and 11 pieces 4 inches long.

3 Glue the shorter wires between a tissue paper leaf and a textured paper leaf with PVA adhesive. Coat the leaves with a solution of 50 percent water and 50 percent all-purpose glue. Leave to dry.

MAKING THE NECKLACE

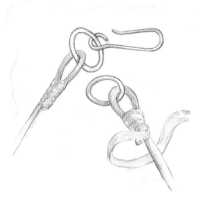

4 Use the point of an awl or bradawl to mark veins on the top (the textured paper side) of the leaf. Serrate the edges of the leaves. Arrange in groups of three. Bind the leaf trios with ¼ inch strips of tissue paper or textured paper, gluing as you go to secure. Cover the berry stalks in the same way.

1 Bind the leaf branches and the berries, gluing as you go, to form a necklace approximately 16 inches long.

2 Attach the hook to one jump ring. Bend over one of the stem wires at each end to form a loop, add the rings and bind the stem end with paper strips.

DECORATIVE CANISTER

This project takes its inspiration from traditional African handicrafts, in which intricately patterned strips are woven to fit snugly over canisters. We have simplified the task by gluing.

YOU WILL NEED
•
Beads and findings
- I ounce red rocaille beads, size 8/0
- 2½ ounces black rocaille beads, size 8/0
- Approximately 20 orange rocaille beads, size 6/0
- Approximately 13 bells
- 4 × 25mm black tubular beads
- I large decorative bead
- I head pin
- Silk thread
- Waxed beading thread
Other equipment
- Small beading loom
- Scissors
- Beading needle
- 25 inches fine black cord
- Clear, all-purpose glue
- Canister
- Round-nosed pliers
- Small nail
- Hammer
- File or sandpaper

MAKING THE PANEL

1 Thread the loom with 30 warp threads, each approximately 20 inches long (see pages 58–59 for loom work instructions).

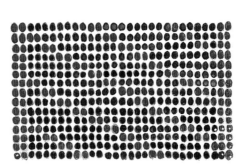

2 Follow the pattern to bead a strip in red and black rocailles long enough to wrap around the canister. Ours has a circumference of about 2½ inches. Cut the strip from the loom and finish off the tails securely. (See the project on pages 84–85 for basic loomwork techniques.)

3 Cut the warp threads close to the last rows of beads and apply glue along both cut edges.

4 For the top row, take a new length of thread through a few red rocailles along one edge, bringing it out through the end bead. Pick up one black rocaille, take the working thread under the thread between the rows and back through the black rocaille. Pick up two black rocailles and take the working thread under the thread between the next two red rocailles.

5 Repeat along the top row and finish off the working thread by running it back through several red rocailles before cutting off.

6 Attach a new length of thread to the bottom edge, running it through about three red rocailles before bringing it out at the bottom edge.

7 Pick up five black rocailles, one red rocaille, one orange rocaille, and a bell. Take the thread back up through the orange, red, and black rocailles and weave it between the row of red rocailles on the bottom edge, bringing it out after the seventh rocaille. Repeat to make another drop.

8 Repeat step 7 until you have worked evenly spaced drops around the bottom edge. The distance between the drops will vary according to the size of the canister and the length of the loomwork strip.

9 When the drops are completed, finish off the working thread and glue the strip around the canister.

DECORATING THE LID

1 Pierce a hole in the middle with a nail and hammer. File smooth. Put an orange rocaille and a large bead on a head pin, take it through the hole, and turn a loop.

2 Cut the fine cord into two equal pieces and use one length to pick up one orange rocaille, one black tube, one orange rocaille, one black tube, and one orange rocaille.

3 Take the other piece of cord through the first orange rocaille, pick up one black tube, one orange rocaille, one black tube, and take the cord through the last orange rocaille on the first piece of cord.

4 Adjust the lengths of cord so that all four ends are equal, then form into a square. Tie a bell at each side. Position the square around the central bead and glue it to the lid.

INDEX

ACKNOWLEDGEMENTS

Unless otherwise specified, all bead projects made by **Alexandra Kidd**.

Daisy Vest 108–9; Shoe Patches 100–11; Harlequin Mask 116–7; Picture Frame 118–9. **Judy Fitzgerald**

Blackberry Necklace 122–23. **Deidre Hawkins**

Painted wooden beads 7; Design fundamentals, middle 10; Homemade Beads, painted wooden and coconut shell 12–3; Single Strands 20; Red & Blue Stranded Set 24–5; Tassel Necklace 26–7; Novelty Earrings 44–5. **Monica Peiser**

Pearl-studded Pincushion 100–1; Decorated Cushion 104–5; Velvet Evening Bag 106–7. **Melanie Williams**

Design Fundamentals, upper left, 10; Using polymer clay, upper left 15; Moon & Stars Necklace 22–3; Knotted Necklace 28–9; Swivel Necklace 46. **Sara Withers**

Beads supplied by:

The London Bead Co.
25 Chalk Farm Rd.
London NW1 UK

Creative Bead Imports
255 South Terrace
South Fremantle
Western Australia

Bojangles
Old Cottage
Appleton, Abingdon
Oxon UK

Ceramic backgrounds made by: **Christine Constance, Romilly Graham**

The author would like to thank Jonathan, Fay, John and Jim for all their support.